Christ and
the Church

"This is a great mystery: but I speak concerning Christ and the church."

—Ephesians 5:32 KJV

"The Lord Jesus is the Head of the Church, which is composed of all His true disciples, and in Him is invested supremely all power for its government."

—Southern Baptist Theological Seminary,
Abstract of Principles, Article XIV, 1858

Christ and
the Church

*An Exposition of Ephesians
with special application to some present issues*

by

DALE MOODY

*Professor of Christian Theology
The Southern Baptist Theological Seminary
Louisville, Kentucky*

WM. B. EERDMANS PUBLISHING CO., GRAND RAPIDS, MICH.

PREFACE

Much of the material in this exposition has been a part of my expository preaching for several years, and it is now offered in publication in response to the request of people in many places. In 1961 Baptist gatherings in Ft. Worth, Texas; Macon, Georgia; Glorieta, New Mexico; and Eagle Eyrie, Virginia, extracted a promise that it would be put in print, but the pressure of other concerns has delayed the final copy.

It is hoped that the technical scholar will be gentle in his criticism, for this exposition is intended only as a bridge between exegesis and the increasing interest of the average Christian in biblical study. With this purpose, the reader is introduced immediately to the text. Background matters and theological summaries are introduced at the appropriate places in the exposition.

The exposition is based on the original language, but Greek words are transliterated and translated so that those without knowledge of Greek will not be hindered. The RSV is quoted most of the time, but in several places preference is given to other translations. If any departure from the RSV is not indicated, with the standard abbreviations, the translation is that of the author.

May those who read find the same joy as does this writer in pondering this heavenly letter.

Dale Moody

CONTENTS

Preface   7

THE SALUTATION (Ephesians 1:1-2)   11

1   THE WORSHIP OF GOD (1:3-23)   15
    Praise (1:3-14)   16
    Prayer (1:15-23)   28

2   THE WORKMANSHIP OF GOD (2:1-22)   40
    The Work of Resurrection (2:1-10)   41
    The Work of Reconciliation (2:11-22)   51

3   THE WISDOM OF GOD (3:1-21)   64
    The Purpose of God (3:1-13)   65
    The Power of God (3:14-21)   74

4   THE CHRISTIAN CALLING (4:1–5:20)   86
    The Call to Walk Worthily (4:1-16)   87
    The Call to Walk Differently (4:17-24)   96
    The Call to Walk in Love (4:25–5:2)   100
    The Call to Walk in the Light (5:3-14)   104
    The Call to Walk Carefully (5:15-20)   110

5 THE CHRISTIAN HOUSEHOLD (5:21—6:9)   115
    Wives and Husbands (5:21-24)   117
    Children and Parents (6:1-4)   127
    Slaves and Masters (6:5-9)   131

6 THE CHRISTIAN CONFLICT (6:10-20)   135
    The Enemy (6:11-13)   136
    The Equipment (6:14-17)   141
    The Endurance (6:18-20)   145

   CONCLUSION (6:21-24)   152
    The Bearer of the Letter (6:21-22)   152
    The Benediction (6:23-24)   153

THE SALUTATION
(Ephesians 1:1-2)

The letter to the Ephesians begins: "Paul, an apostle of Christ Jesus by the will of God" (1:1). Until modern times the reality of this authorship has been unquestioned. It was assumed that Paul wrote both Colossians and Ephesians during his Roman imprisonment and sent them together by Tychicus to the respective churches (6:21f.). With great erudition this point of view has been defended by the Anglican scholar F. J. A. Hort.[1] The Roman Catholic scholar Heinrich Schlier, who has produced one of the most thorough studies of the Greek text,[2] and other defenders of the historic view, have added very little to Hort's studies on authorship.

The greatest challenge to the historic view comes from the Baptist New Testament scholar E. J. Goodspeed, who dates the document in the tenth decade, when Onesimus, on reading Acts, set out to collect all the letters of Paul, with Colossians and Philemon as his core. On completing the collection from seven different churches, he arranged the letters according to their length and made a digest as a preface to the Pauline corpus.[3] This digest was based on Colossians but other materials were added from the various letters. The digest as preface is the Ephesian letter, according to Goodspeed. C. Leslie Mitton, an English Methodist New Testament scholar, has elaborated Goodspeed's theory,[4] but

[1] *Prolegomena to St. Paul's Epistles to the Romans and Ephesians.*
[2] *Der Brief an die Epheser.*
[3] *The Meaning of Ephesians.*
[4] *The Epistle to the Ephesians.*

11

it has not gained general acceptance. One of the most recent studies rejects it.[5] Ephesians may be related to Colossians much as Romans to Galatians. One is a calm rewriting of the other. It is not the purpose of this exposition to be preoccupied with this complicated problem, but either view leaves Ephesians at the very peak of Paul's theology. From this peak the most earthly problems can be viewed from "the heavenly places" where their answers and solutions are to be found. There is hardly a major issue of contemporary Christianity that does not come up for clear consideration and for a most majestic approach toward the solution. What Romans meant in the time of the Reformation, this letter means in this time of renewal. He who ponders these brief pages with heart and mind open will never be satisfied with himself and the present predicament of the Church in the modern world. He will be satisfied only as this lofty vision becomes more and more a historical reality.

The address "to the saints who are faithful in Christ Jesus" is involved in the problem of authorship, but the manuscript evidence is against the reading "who are of Ephesus and faithful." It is very difficult to defend this with the Chester Beatty papyri of the third century and the Vatican and Sinai Manuscripts of the fourth century all against it. This is another technical problem, but the Nestle Greek text and standard textual studies are very much of one mind on the answer. The RSV is no doubt correct in relegating the reading to a footnote.

The greeting (1:2), found in all the Pauline letters, combines the ancient Semitic idea of peace (*shalom*) with the distinctive Christian belief in "God our Father and the Lord Jesus Christ." God's fatherhood in Ephesians may be compared to a circle composed of all who confess Jesus Christ as Lord, with Christ at the very center. God is Father of the Lord Jesus Christ by nature and from all eternity (1:3, 17),

[5] Henry Chadwick, in *Peake's Commentary on the Bible*, edited by Matthew Black and H. H. Rowley, pp. 980f.

but he is also Father of all Christians by adoption (1:2; 2:18; 3:14; 4:6; 5:20). It is possible that some passages reach beyond this redemptive fatherhood to the creative fatherhood that would include all that is not God (3:14; 4:6), but this is not the central thrust in Ephesians. Creative fatherhood is more likely to be found in I Corinthians 8:6 ("the Father, from whom are all things and from whom we exist"). In Ephesians and for the problems of present Christianity, it is important to put emphasis on the major theme of this letter: God is Father of all who confess Jesus Christ as Lord. In this one family of God men are called to live as brothers.

The "Lord Jesus Christ," who makes all men brothers, is the shortest creed of the Christian faith. Indeed, it is correct to say we have no creed but Christ. As Lord he is exalted to the right hand of God, the place of authority; as Jesus he is the historic person who partook of our humanity to make us one new man; and as Christ he is God's anointed to fulfill the purpose of all human history. The early hymn of the servant in Philippians 2:5-11 concludes with a summary of this purpose. Through the movements of humiliation (2:6-8) and exaltation (2:9-11) the purpose of God is to bring all men to "confess that Jesus Christ is Lord, to the glory of God the Father" (2:11).

Chapter One:

THE WORSHIP OF GOD
(Ephesians 1:3-23)

One of the leading religious philosophers of our time has raised a jolting question: "Is modern theology atheistic?"[1] In a penetrating article under this title the legacy of Greek thought is challenged and a call to return to the living God of the Bible, as "a Being worthy of worship," is sounded forth. It is "the inadequate and arbitrary categories of Greek thought," transmitted to modern thought through Immanuel Kant, that account for much of our "tongue-tied stammering about God and the social irrelevance of its message," says the University of Wisconsin professor. The author gets to the bottom of our needs when he declares: "What man needs is not a God to serve him but a God he can serve." It is the purpose of this chapter to point to God as "a Being worthy of worship" and to his Church as a body to which it is worth belonging.

The daily prayers of the synagogue, since pre-Christian times, have begun with three blessings and ended with three thanksgivings. Blessing God is a sacred bridge between the worship of the synagogue and the worship of the Church, and the former no doubt influenced the latter. The great difference is that Christians, who believe that Jesus is the Messiah, bless God through Christ in the Spirit, but the Hallelujah note is the

[1] A. Campbell Garnett, *The Christian Century*, May 31, 1961, pp. 680-682.

15

very heart of all biblical worship (cf. Ps. 111-117; Rev. 19:1-6) and of all worship based on the Bible.

On this foundation belief in the Holy Trinity is based, so that "the doxology" comes spontaneously to be the theme of all true worship.

> Praise God, from whom all blessings flow;
> Praise Him, all creatures here below;
> Praise Him above, ye heavenly host;
> Praise Father, Son, and Holy Ghost. Amen.

These are no idle words to be sung as Christians draw near to the throne of grace.

To this may be added also the *Gloria Patri*:

> Glory be to the Father, and to the Son, and to the Holy Ghost;
> As it was in the beginning, is now and ever shall be,
>   world without end. Amen. Amen.

When such words in song no longer spring forth from the hearts of the worshiping congregation, deadness has indeed set in. Ephesians 1:3-14 will do much to revive the worship of the triune God when it is rightly understood.

PRAISE (1:3-14)

The translation of the ASV makes this passage one long sentence, and it is possible that forms of liturgical prayer constitute the basis of this doxology of the early Church. A recent analysis has concluded that the same forms are to be found behind I Peter 1:3-12, although Ephesians 1:3-14 has followed them more closely.[2] Even the casual reader will note that the two passages open with the same phrase of ten words. It may be helpful to translate the proposed reconstruction, remembering that the original Greek is more impressive.

> Blessed art thou, the God and Father of our Lord Jesus Christ
>   who has blessed us with every spiritual blessing in the
>   heavenly places in Christ,
>   who has chosen us in him before the foundation of the
>   world,

[2] J. Coutts, *New Testament Studies*, III, 115-127.

who predestined us to sonship through Jesus Christ according to the good pleasure of thy will
to the praise of thy glory.

According to thy grace by which thou didst bestow grace on us
in the Beloved,
in whom we have the forgiveness of our trespasses,
in whom we received redemption through his blood,
in whom we were allotted our inheritance
according to the good pleasure of thy will
to the praise of thy glory.

In whom, by the Holy Spirit,
we heard the gospel of salvation;
we believed the word of truth;
we were sealed to the redemption of the possession,
according to the good pleasure of thy will,
to the praise of thy glory.

This reconstruction must of course be tentative, but it is perfect trinitarian praise of God. With this the present expanded
form will be considered.

The work of the Father (1:3-6). The first part of the great
doxology is focused on God the Father of our Lord Jesus
Christ (cf. II Cor. 1:3; Rom. 15:6; I Pet. 1:3; Rev. 1:6). Had
the passage done no more than call people to worship God,
with no description of the God they were called to worship,
strange things could have resulted. Possibly the people would
run off to a god factory to purchase an idol for the house or
go to the temple to offer pagan sacrifices. The situation is well
described by Paul: "For although there may be so-called gods
in heaven or on earth — as indeed there are many 'gods' and
many 'lords' — yet for us there is one God, the Father from
whom are all things and for whom we exist, and one Lord
Jesus Christ, through whom are all things and through whom
we exist" (I Cor. 8:5f.).

We are called to bless "the God and Father of our Lord
Jesus Christ who has blessed us in Christ with every spiritual
blessing in the heavenly places" (1:3). Even the philosopher
would have misunderstood an undefined call to worship God.

Today, with polytheism left behind, a collection of the concep-
tions of God is bewildering.[3] As the philosopher would approach the idea of God through value, the Bible would focus
on his benefits.

> Bless the Lord, O my soul;
>   and all that is within me,
>   bless his holy name!
> Bless the Lord, O my soul;
>   and forget not all his benefits (Ps. 103:1).

Look now at some of his benefits.

He has blessed us (1:3)! This is the first reason to bless
him. He has "blessed us with every spiritual blessing." It
has been suggested that "every" describes the *comprehensive-
ness* of the blessing and "spiritual" the *character* of the blessing.[4] "Every" blessing allows no limit. In Christ God freely
gives "all things" (Rom. 8:32). As an early hymn says: "All
things are yours, whether Paul or Apollos or Cephas or the
world or life or death or the present or the future, all are
yours; and you are Christ's and Christ is God's" (I Cor. 3:21f.).

The character of the blessings makes them "spiritual." They
are bestowed in the spiritual realm, "in the heavenly places"
(*en tois epouraniois*), a phrase found only in Ephesians (1:3,
20; 2:6; 3:10; 6:12). The thought stimulated in the first read-
ers was perhaps in terms of the atmosphere of heaven having
come down to earth "in Christ." It was not necessary to take
a rocket ride to get into this realm; it required repentance and
a turning to Christ.

In the long sentence (1:3-14) the phrases "in Christ," "in
him," and "in whom" appear eleven times and in the whole
letter at least thirty times. This is the special realm of God's
revealing and redeeming activity, for "in Christ" man comes
to know God as God makes himself known to man (cf. Gal.
4:9). In Christ a new beginning is made. "Therefore, if
any one is in Christ, he is a new creation; the old has passed
away, behold, the new has come. All this is from God, who

---

[3] E. S. Brightman, *A Philosophy of Religion*, pp. 133-161.
[4] *The Interpreter's Bible, ad loc.*

through Christ reconciled us to himself and gave us the ministry of reconciliation; that is, in Christ God was reconciling the world to himself, not counting their trespasses against them, and entrusting to us the message of reconciliation" (II Cor. 5:17-19).

God also chose us (1:4)! He chose us before (*pro*) creation to stand before (*katenōpion*) him. The choice was neither in creation nor after creation but "before the foundation of the world." It was before creation, not the accident of evolution, not an afterthought in history. In both creation and redemption the purpose of God is plain prior to all natural process and human history, for he is the transcendent and triune God.

The purpose of this prior choice is "that we should be holy and blameless before him in love" (cf. Col. 1:22). "Holy and blameless' (*hagios* and *amōmos*) are sacrificial words (cf. Lev. 1:3, 10), and the best summary of the sacrificial life is Paul's plea in Romans 12:1f.

> I appeal to you therefore, brethren, by the mercies of God, to present your bodies as a living sacrifice, holy and acceptable to God, which is your spiritual worship.

He has called us to be blameless, without blemish as a sacrificial animal. God requires the best, not the second best in devotion and service.

God then *pre*destined us (1:5)! He knew where he was going before he started out, but this is no act of blind fate. God is the living God of purpose and plan who works by love. "He destined us in love to be his sons through Jesus Christ." It is "in love" and "through Jesus Christ" that we are predestined. Our destiny is the same as the destiny of Christ, namely glory, because we are "in Christ." The faith of a true theology and the fate of a false astrology should never be confused. Man's destiny is not due to his lucky star but to God's grace lavished upon him in Christ.

Sonship is the very opposite of slavery. Paul's great Galatian letter is especially concerned with this theme. Galatians 4:1-11 describes the drama by which "God sent forth his Son" to be born of a woman so that "the Spirit of his Son" could be sent forth to make us sons of God (1-7). Deliverance from slavery to sonship is so great that a return from sonship to slavery is sheer folly (4:8-11; 5:1). The status of sonship makes redeemed sinners "heirs of God and fellow heirs with Christ, provided we suffer with him in order that we may also be glorified with him" (Rom. 8:17).

The very mention of election and predestination sends cold chills through many sincere people. The picture that comes up before their minds is that of an arbitrary tyrant sitting on a throne with the multitudes of men marching by. If one has the wrong number he is in trouble. To number seven he says: "you go to heaven"; but to number six: "you are in a fix." It is impossible to clear Augustine and Calvin at this point, for their systems do suggest this picture to the pious mind.

Recent revival in biblical theology has changed the picture, but most of the new insight on election and predestination has not been passed on to non-scholars. H. H. Rowley rightly chose the occasion of lectures in Spurgeon's College to expound *The Biblical Doctrine of Election.*[5] Spurgeon himself was too inclined toward a rigid Calvinism that threatened the missionary theology of William Carey, but Rowley makes a major contribution to missionary theology by recovering the biblical idea of election in terms of God's purpose for all nations.

Some have thought that the Christocentric theology of Karl Barth recovers the biblical view, but Barth is baffling.[6] His approach from Christ through the community to the Christian is no doubt correct, but there are places where he seems to draw the conclusion of universal salvation. All are indeed lost in Adam, but does he also mean all men are in Christ and will be saved? Perhaps the publication of his eschatology will make this clearer than his treatise on election.

It is interesting to note that the Orthodox Creed (1678)

---

[5] See Bibliography.
[6] *Church Dogmatics*, Vol. II/2, pp. 3-506.

of English Baptists speaks of "Jesus, whom he elected before the foundation of the world," who "is called God's elect," and says that "God the father gave his elected and beloved son, for a covenant to the people."[7] It is unfortunate that the Second London Confession (1677) finally became the basis of Baptist unity, for it retained too much of the rigid Calvinism that resists missions and evangelism. It is Christ that is elected and predestined, so that all in Christ are elected and predestined with him. This is missionary and evangelistic to the core, and this is the point of view in Romans 8:29f. and Ephesians 1:5.

The work of the Son (1:7-12). God has bestowed his grace "in the Beloved." The Greek of Ephesians 1:6 could be translated "to the praise of the glory of his grace with which he graced us in the Beloved." The noun *charis* (grace) and the verb *echaritōsen* (he freely bestowed) are built on the same stem. The KJV "made us accepted" is too far from the Greek meaning. Grace is the groundwork of all Paul's thought, and it comes up again for detailed consideration in Ephesians 2:1-10.

The Beloved is a messianic title applied to Christ in Mark 1:11: "Thou art my Son, the Beloved." The perfect participle *ēgapēmenos* (the beloved) in Ephesians 1:6 designates Jesus as the center of God's love and the sphere in which believers come to know this love. The major points on this work of God in Christ are in the three *kata* (according) clauses, and around these this part of the praise will be summarized.

It is first according to his grace (1:7). "In him we have redemption through his blood, the forgiveness of our trespasses, according to the riches of his grace which he lavished upon us" (1:7f.; cf. Col. 1:14). Redemption (*apolutrōsis*) has reference to both the power and the price that sets men free from sin. Even land is redeemed in Israel (Lev. 25:25-27, 47-49; Num. 18:15). The primary pictures drawn from the

---

[7] W. L. Lumpkin, *Baptist Confessions of Faith* (Philadelphia: The Judson Press, 1959), p. 302.

Old Testament have in mind the deliverance from Egypt and later from Babylon (Ex. 15:13; Deut. 7:8; Isa. 48:20; 52:9). In the New Testament the institution of slavery is used to call attention to the great cost by which freedom is purchased. *Lutros* is the price paid to set a slave free, and *apolutrōsis* is the act by which the emancipation is accomplished. For the believer in Christ the price is "the blood" of Christ and the act is his death (Acts 20:28; I Cor. 6:20; Rom. 3:24; Heb. 9:22; I Pet. 1:18f.; Rev. 5:9).

Forgiveness (*aphesis*) means the release from that which binds. We are released from the debt of our trespasses (*paraptōmatōn*), a word which means to slip or fall from the right way. Man has taken the wrong road and finds himself at the end of a dead-end street in need of forgiveness. The debt is removed at great cost.

Lavishing (*eperisseusen*) and freely bestowing (*echaritōsen*) mean much the same, but *perisseuō* has the picture of grace overflowing like a river. As the Father bestows his love he also floods the faithful in Christ Jesus. Christ is the channel that irrigates the fields of God. Faith opens the flood gates (Rom. 5:1-5). Grace abounding is a dominant theme in Ephesians (1:7, 18; 2:4, 7; 3:8, 16), as in other Pauline writings (Col. 1:27; 2:2; II Cor. 8:9; Rom. 2:4; 9:23; 11:33).

The flood of grace comes not as a catastrophe but as the spring rains "in all wisdom and prudence." Wisdom (*sophia*) is the ability to apprehend first principles or the ultimate reality, and prudence (*phronēsis*) is the right application of these principles to specific situations. God in his grace reveals himself and redeems man according to the principles of wisdom and in the most practical way.

In the second place, God's revealing and redeeming activity in Christ is "according to his good pleasure" (1:9; cf. Col. 1:9). Good pleasure, as in the KJV, is much nearer the meaning of the Greek word *eudokia* than the word "purpose" in the translation of the RSV, for it suggests both the good will and the sovereignty of God in the salvation of man. It was "according to his good pleasure" that "the mystery of his will" was made known, for "the mystery of his will" (1:9) is the same as "the good pleasure of his will" (1:5; cf. Col. 1:26; 2:2; 4:3). His good pleasure is a mystery because it was once hidden and is now made known as God graciously unveils his purpose and opens the eyes of man to behold his revelation (Rom. 15:25).

It is the mystery "which he set forth in Christ as a plan for the fulness of time" (1:9). This "plan" (*oikonomia*), translated dispensation in the KJV and ASV, is God's *economy* projected for the redemption of man. It is the way God manages for his household (cf. I Cor. 4:1f.; 9:17; Tit. 1:7; I Pet. 4:10). It was in "the fulness of time" (*plērōma tou chronou*, Gal. 4:4) that "God sent forth his Son . . . to redeem," and "the plan for the fulness of time (*eis oikonomian tou plērōmatos tōn kairōn*). *Chronos* is that calendar time in which all days and years are the same, but *kairos* is this empty time filled with grace and meaning by the revealing and redeeming activity of God.

His purpose is "to unite all things in him, things in heaven and things on earth" (1:10). This unity is the restoration of harmony to God's creation that has been disturbed by the discords of sin. The infinitive *anakephalaiōsasthai* (to unite), which was used to denote the sum of figures or an address, defines the mystery of God's will. God wills that all the mysterious ways in his redemptive plans lead to one goal, Christ. This "sums it up." It includes the whole realm of his creation (all things, *ta panta*) in the drama of redemption.

Irenaeus of Lyon (c. 180) based his doctrine of "recapitulation" on this text, for when Christ "was incarnate and made man, he recapitulated [or summed up] in himself the long line of the human race, procuring for us salvation thus summarily, so that what we had lost in Adam, that is, the being in the image and likeness of God, that we should regain in Christ Jesus" (*Adv. haer.* III.XVIII, Bettenson).

A third *kata* clause says that God's revealing and redeeming activity is according to his purpose (1:11). According to God's purpose the redeemed are made his portion. The KJV mistranslates and the RSV misses completely the idea clearly rendered in the ASV. It is not that "we have obtained an inheritance" (KJV), but "we were made a heritage" (*eklērō-thēmen*, 1:11). The verb comes from *klēros* (lot, portion), and the idea is that of Deuteronomy 32:9 ("For the Lord's portion is his people, Jacob his allotted heritage"). Compare Deuteronomy 4:20; 9:29. Our word clergy comes from the word *klēros*, a clergyman being one to whom a portion of God's flock is allotted. They are his charge (*klēros*, I Pet. 5:3).

According to God's purpose the redeemed in Christ are also predestined (1:12). It is by predestination that the redeemed are made God's portion. This again brings up that much misused word that was discussed in 1:5, *proorisas* (having predestined), here *prooristhetes* (having been predestined). God's portion, his people, has already been marked off, and God works in "all things after the counsel of his will" (ASV) to acquire this possession. His counsel (*boulē*) is his plan (Acts 2:23; 4:28; 13:36; 20:27). Predestination to sonship (1:5) and predestination to be God's portion or heritage (1:11) mean the same. In both God would possess his own. This is the hope that we have in Christ, and those in Christ are "to live for the praise of his glory."

The work of the Spirit (1:13f.). It is impossible to worship the living God of the New Testament in deep experience and with true understanding when the Holy Spirit is neglected. Indeed, it is impossible even to know him in the fulness of his revelation and in the benefits of his redemption if men "have never even heard that there is a Holy Spirit" (Acts 19:2). This is the plight of all too many today.

Perhaps the present passage may point some in the right direction. Note first the preparation for a personal Pentecost, if this is the right way to put the experience in popular language. These early Christians first "heard the word of truth" (1:13). Colossians 1:5 speaks of "the word of truth" as that which tells of the hope laid up in heaven. Epaphras had preached "the gospel" which was "bearing fruit and growing" in "the whole world" (Col. 1:6).

This "word of truth" is the very opposite of the hodge-podge being preached in the Lycus Valley. Ephesians 1:13 describes it as "the gospel of your salvation." This is the same as "the gospel of God" (I Thess. 2:9), "the gospel of the glory of Christ" (II Cor. 4:4), and "the gospel of the grace of God" (Acts 20:24). It is primarily good news about God, but it is for "your salvation."

The second step toward salvation and the experience of the Holy Spirit is that they "believed in him" (1:13), i.e., Christ. This may mean either that Christ is the object or the realm of their belief, perhaps both. They believed in order to be in him and are now in him. It does *not* mean that they were in him before they "believed in him." It would be necessary to say they were in him before they heard, if this were true, for *en hō* (in whom) is used in each case.

One would prefer to avoid controversy while expounding an epistle on Christian unity, but current appeal to this passage to justify infant baptism calls for comment.[8] Infants born into a Christian household do have some relation to the body of Christ that infants born of pagans do not (I Cor. 7:14). The early Church was perhaps right in making a distinction between the children as catechumens and the faithful, but they were children not yet born, in the womb of Mother Church, stored in the barn but not yet brought forth to the threshing floor.[9]

Belief is clearly defined in the New Testament as that which one does for himself, not as that which another does for him. An early confession says (Rom. 10:9f.):

> If you confess with your lips that Jesus is Lord
> and believe in your heart that God raised him from the dead,
> you will be saved.

[8] John A. T. Robinson, "Our Present Position in the Light of the Bible," in *Becoming a Christian*, edited by Basil Minchin, pp. 51-53; *The Interpreter's Bible*, ad loc.

[9] E. C. Whitaker, *Documents of the Baptismal Liturgy*, pp. 50f., 90-96.

> For man believes with his heart and so is justified
> and he confesses with his lips
> and so is saved.

There is not the slightest suggestion that another can do this as his sponsor or substitute, and there is not until the beginning of the third century A.D. any evidence for infant baptism.[10]

The promise of a personal Pentecost is fulfilled when one has "heard" and "believed." Every household baptism in the New Testament is clearly described as believer's baptism. The members of "the household of Stephanas" were such as could devote themselves "to the service of the saints," a strange activity indeed for infants (I Cor. 1:16; 16:15). Lydia perhaps had no husband, so the members of her household, baptized with her, would be household slaves (Acts 16:15). The household of the Philippian jailer who were baptized with him also "rejoiced" that he had "believed in God" (Acts 16:-31-34). The household of Crispus also "believed in the Lord" before they were baptized (Acts 18:8; I Cor. 1:14).

After hearing and believing they "were sealed with the promised Holy Spirit." The sealing of the Spirit is today a debated issue in the Church of England. One theologian with "low church" leanings has been contending that the seal of the Spirit is given in baptism, and he has made a major contribution by bringing so much material to light.[11] Another scholar, an Anglican monk with "high church" leanings, has replied in a defense of the traditional view that the Holy Spirit is given in confirmation, at the time hands are laid on the head by the bishop.[12]

To this writer, who has learned much from the discussion, both authors have committed what may be called a punctiliar fallacy, i.e., confining the work of the Spirit too much to one point. The Holy Spirit, in normal Christian experience, works before, in, and after baptism. Baptism *with* the laying on of

---

[10] Kurt Aland, *Did the Early Church Baptize Infants?*
[11] G. W. H. Lampe, *The Seal of the Spirit.*
[12] L. S. Thornton, *Confirmation.*

hands, as even the Philadelphia Confession of Faith of Baptists holds, should be a crucial moment, but the Church of England has created an insoluble problem by separating baptism from the laying on of hands by twelve to fourteen years in their practice of infant baptism.

All too many Baptists turn to the opposite extreme and speak as if *all* the work of the Spirit takes place *before* baptism. This shallow "mere symbolism" has happily been corrected by careful study of the New Testament.[13] It is hoped that these brief remarks will at least arouse interest in the relationship between the Holy Spirit and baptism, for that is perhaps the setting of this passage on the seal of the Spirit (see also 4:30 and II Cor. 1:21f.). The symbol of sealing was an Oriental custom, and the sign and seal of a Christian was and is that he has received the Spirit! As the Christ is the One anointed with the Spirit in a special way (Acts 10:38), so a Christian is one who has at least received the Spirit in some way (Acts 11:26; 26:28; I Pet. 4:16).

As one receives the seal of the Spirit he also receives the "earnest" (*arrabōn*) of the Spirit. *Arrabōn*, which in the LXX is a pledge (Gen. 38:17-20), means more than the "guarantee" in the RSV (Eph. 1:14; II Cor. 1:22; 5:5). A word associated with Phoenician traders, it is a "down payment" that binds the bargain and guarantees the full payment later. As it is applied to the "earnest of our inheritance" (KJV, ASV), it perhaps means that the believing Christian has received the first portion of the promised Spirit and has the guarantee that the rest will be received at "the day of redemption" (Eph. 4:30). This is strengthened by the fact that II Corinthians 5:5 uses the *arrabōn* of the Spirit as a guarantee that when the human spirit leaves the human body at death it departs to "a house not made with hands, eternal in the heavens" (II Cor. 5:1).[14]

Another possibility should, however, be mentioned. It seems that "inheritance" has reference to God's portion, his

---

[13] G. R. Beasley-Murray, *Baptism in the New Testament*.
[14] A detailed discussion may be found in my forthcoming book *The Hope of Glory*.

people in Ephesians 1:11 ("we were made a heritage") and Ephesians 1:18 ("his inheritance in the saints"). The translation of the ASV also renders the next clause "unto the redemption of God's own possession" in Ephesians 1:14. Compare the New English Bible: "When God has redeemed what is his own." It is not an easy decision to make, but the phrase "our inheritance" tips the scales in favor of the RSV ("our inheritance until we acquire possession of it"). This teaching is found in both Deuteronomy 32:8 and Colossians 1:12 both of which are in the background of this passage. If this interpretation be correct, both man (Deut. 32:8; Col. 1: 12; Eph. 1:14) and God (Deut. 32:9; Eph. 1:11, 18) have an inheritance in the promised land, the portion of God's people being God and God's portion being his people (cf. I Pet. 2:9). This leads to prayer as the second form of worship.

PRAYER (1:15-23)

Twice in the Ephesian letter prayers appear, a sure sign that the work sprang out of the worship of the early Church. In this paragraph the prayer is one for knowledge, and it is the profoundest passage in the whole Bible for exploring the resources of the inner man. In times when so much is objective and lifeless, it is good to turn within and plumb the depths of the soul in its relation to God. The prayer may be divided into two parts: spiritual knowledge (1:15-18) and spiritual power (1:19-23).

Spiritual knowledge (1:15-19). Reinhold Niebuhr, in one of the best books he has written, speaks of the dialogues of the soul or self with itself, with others, and with God.[15] In few places may one find freedom and the reality of God presented with more penetration, and the insights are fundamentally those found in biblical realism. In this Ephesian passage the three dialogues appear, although the order is different.

The passage speaks first of the self in relation to others: "I

---

[15] *The Self and the Dramas of History,* pp. 3-72.

have heard of your faith in the Lord Jesus and your love toward all the saints" (1:15). Even the faith in the Lord Jesus needs to be understood as a personal knowledge of a presence that is nearer than the Jesus of history. It is the Lord Jesus! When faith identifies the Jesus of history with the Lord of glory Christianity is born and the first great stride to a doctrine of the Trinity is taken, and when this connection is severed the Christian faith will sink. This is the faith by which the saints live and die.

All who have faith in the Lord Jesus are Christian saints. Of course, there are those unusual souls who climb higher than others in search of spiritual satisfaction, but "the saints" here means all Christians. The recipients of this letter had "love toward all the saints." Even though some ancient manuscripts do not have the phrase "your love," it is well to give some attention to this true characteristic of a saint. W. O. Carver frequently spoke to his students about an attack that was once made on his doctrinal soundness, a thing that often happened in the life of this unusual man, and the doubt about his orthodoxy grew out of an article on "love toward all the saints." Certain "exclusive brethren" felt such belief was a threat to their "historic position."

Love (agapē) is the willingness to share with others all that one is and has. Emil Brunner has said: "Love does not ask what is mine and what is thine: it does not render to the other what is his due, what belongs to him 'by right,' but gives of its own, gives precisely that to which the other has no right."[16] Justice gives to each man his due, but love gives to man what is not his due; justice asks: "What is mine and what is thine?" but love says: "What is mine is thine." Much of the tension within and without the Church springs from a cold justice severed from the warmth of love.

The second dialogue is with God. God is here called "the Father of glory" (1:17). In the early Church Christ is called "the Lord of glory" (Jas. 2:1; I Cor. 2:8), and it is possible

---

[16] *Justice and the Social Order,* p. 17.

that Jesus is here looked upon as the *Shekinah* glory, the mode by which God makes his presence known among his people. God is then called the Father of the one who is the *Shekinah* glory, the one in whom God came to dwell among his people.[17]

God's glory and God's gift are closely linked, for it is through his presence in Christ that the saints are able to receive "a spirit of wisdom and revelation in the knowledge of him." In the fellowship between the Holy Spirit of God and the human spirit wisdom and revelation are given. Wisdom is the right understanding of reality, and revelation is the unveiling of this reality. Here is the ultimate reality on which all things rest, the first principle behind all things visible and invisible, namely Christ. To know him is to know the ultimate, and to be related to him is to anchor the soul in that which does not pass away.

The third dialogue is of the soul with itself (1:19). Augustine was weak in his emphasis on the soul in relation to others, but on the relation between the soul and itself and on the relation of the soul to God he was strong. In his search for himself, as recorded in his *Soliloquies*, appears the following (II. 7):

> Augustine: Lo, I have prayed to God.
> Reason: Now what do you want to know?
> Augustine: All those things which I prayed for.
> Reason: Sum them up briefly.
> Augustine: I desire to know God and the soul.
> Reason: Nothing more?
> Augustine: Absolutely nothing.

It is passionate longing for God that made him one of the authentic "saints" of all time, and it is amazing how relevant his mysticism is to our scientific age. Science without saints is doomed.

A great Quaker writer, speaking of "the eyes of the heart," says: "I remember sitting down once, when I was a young

---

[17] The *Shekinah* has been discussed in some detail in my article in *The Interpreter's Dictionary of the Bible*.

man, proposing to read this Epistle. I decided that I would not read on until I completely understood the verse I was then reading. I soon found that if I strictly kept that resolution I should never do anything else but read that Epistle!"[18]

When the eyes of his heart are enlightened a man knows three things: his calling, his inheritance, and his power — three so-called "his" clauses. The hope of "his calling" is to renew and reunite the whole creation, visible and invisible, under the Lordship of Jesus Christ: "to unite all things in him, things in heaven and things on earth" (1:10). This is what God intends to do even through men living now in hostile estrangement from him and one another. "His inheritance" is his people. This was previously mentioned in 1:11 ("we were made a heritage," ASV), and the inheritance (*klēronomia*) seems to convey the same thought. The general idea in this passage is that God is calling his people together to be his portion in the promised land (see Deut. 32:9f.), and we need our eyes open to see "Canaan's fair and happy land." What a purpose to know about! What a plan into which one is called to be a part! But some eyes are not yet open, and they grope in darkness. The third clause, "his power," flowers forth to fill the rest of the prayer, the second part. The power that works in Christ works in the Christian.

Spiritual power (1:19b-22). The power of God is exhibited in the spiritual energy by which Christ is exalted and all things are subordinated to him as Lord. The *exaltation* of Christ (1:19b-21) displays both the uncreated and created powers. The uncreated power of God is expressed in four different words: *dunamis* (power), *energeia* (working), strength (*kratos*) and might (*ischus*). *Dunamis* is a general word that includes the totality of the other three. *Energeia* is the power as it goes forth in action, *kratos* is this power grasping and accomplishing the task, and *ischus* is the power inherent that made the going forth and grasping possible.

[18] Rufus Jones, *New Eyes for Invisibles*, p. 10.

It is a picture of a completed action performed by sufficient power.

As Christ was exalted by the uncreated powers of God, so has he been exalted above the created powers which are now hostile to God. They would be gods, but they are by nature "no gods" (Gal. 4:8). Colossians 1:16 speaks of them as "thrones, dominions, principalities and authorities," Ephesians 1:21 as "rule and authority and power and dominion," Romans 8:38 has another list, and there is apparently no end to the names used to describe their nature. Ephesians 1:21 suggests this with the words: "is named, not only in this age, but also in that which is to come." As Paul says: "Indeed there are many 'gods' and many 'lords'" (I Cor. 8:5).

The multiplicity of names, natures, and functions assigned to them has caused some to brush them aside as of little importance for the understanding of Ephesians and the New Testament in general, but this attitude is changing among others most alert to the revival in biblical theology![19]

The *subordination* of all things to the sovereign Lordship of Jesus Christ is the corollary of his exaltation to the right hand of God. The two ideas are already joined in the statement already considered: "far above all rule and authority and power and dominion, and above every name that is named, not only in this age but also in that which is to come" (Eph. 1:21).

His *exaltation* and the *subordination* of all things to him connect the two ages. The "present evil age" (Gal. 1:4) will continue until all powers hostile to the will of God have been subdued, but "the powers of the age to come" (Heb. 6:5) are already at work in the world. The Church as the body of Christ is being built between the ages, and in the Church "the powers of the age to come" are made manifest according to the obedience of her members, the members of Christ's body.

[19] G. B. Caird, *Principalities and Powers;* Heinrich Schlier, *Principalities and Powers in the New Testament.* Caird interprets the powers in a functional rather than in a personal sense.

The town hall view of the Church which reduces the gathering of believers to a secular club falls far short of the New Testament teaching that views the Church as the body of Christ constituted through the work of the Holy Spirit in all who submit to the Lordship of Christ. The interim between the beginning and completion of the body of Christ, the first and second coming of Christ, is not a vacuum. Church history becomes intertwined with secular history, at times entangled and involved to the point of compromise and weakness, but Church history, as the great historians like August Neander and Philip Schaff saw so clearly, belongs more to the stream of salvation history seen in the Bible than to secular history outside the Bible. Church history rightly belongs to *theological* education.

Proof text preaching is often slurred, too often by those who have no texts to support their own unbiblical views, but here are examples of how God's new revelation of himself in the New Testament is seen in the light of the old revelation in the Old Testament. The old is not destroyed but fulfilled, so that Psalm 110:1 ("sit at my right hand") and Psalm 8:6 ("thou hast put all things under his feet") are understood in a deeper and fuller way in the light of the exaltation of Christ and the subordination of all things to his Lordship (1:20, 22).

A more careful consideration of subordination needs to examine three powerful words freighted with meaning. The first is *panta* (all things), found in Psalm 8:6 and mentioned already in Ephesians 1:10f. What does it mean? Before a conclusion is drawn, light may be sought in the companion letter of Colossians. A luminous poem in Colossians 1:15-20 is so important for background to Ephesians 1:10f. and 22f. that it may be reconstructed on the basis of some suggestions made by Eduard Schweizer.[20] With "all things" (*ta panta*) underlined and comments in parentheses, the following arrangement is made of the hymn:

[20] "The Church as the Missionary Body of Christ," *New Testament Studies,* VIII (Oct., 1961), 6-10.

He is the image of the invisible God, the firstborn of all creation, for in him *all things* were created, in heaven and on
earth, (visible and invisible
whether thrones or dominions
or principalities or authorities)
through him and for him *all things* have been created.

And it is he who is before *all things*
and in him *all things* hold together,
and it is he who is the head of the body (the Church) .

He is the beginning, the first born of the dead
(that in everything he might be pre-eminent) ,
for in him all the fullness was pleased to dwell
and through him to reconcile to him *all things*
(whether on earth or in heaven,
making peace through the blood of his cross) .

In each of the three stanzas it is clear that "all things"
means all that does not belong on the side of the Creator and
Savior, all that is not God.   Only God is not subordinated
to Christ, as is also clearly taught in I Corinthians 15:27f.
In pantheism God is all things, but in Scripture all things are
created by God the Creator, the Wholly Other.   The Creator
and Savior must not be confused with the created, and in
Ephesians 1:22f.   Christ, the exalted Lord to whom all things
are made subject, belongs on the side of the Creator and
Savior, for he is the agent of creation and salvation.[21]   No
creature christology can be found here.

After proclaiming the subordination of all things in general
to the Lordship of Christ the passage concentrates on the
subordination of the Church to Christ in particular: "He
has put all things under his feet and has made him head
over all things for the church" (1:22).

Before turning to the two words that are so important for
understanding the nature of the Church, some brief remarks
need to be made on the word *ekklesia,* translated "church."
The concept of the Church as a congregation meeting under
one roof is found in the New Testament.   The New Testament

[21] Franz Mussner, *Christus, das All, und die Kirche.*

references to house churches are perhaps the nearest parallel
(I Cor. 16:19; Col. 4:15; Phil. 2; Rom. 16:5). This local
congregation has been and will ever be the growing point in
the body. As these local "cells" increase and grow in health
the whole body of Christ is made stronger, but when these
cells no longer grow, the health of the whole body of Christ
is endangered. The faithful souls who engage in the labor
of love of a local congregation are the infantry in the army
of Christ. An army may still function without officers, but
without the "foot soldiers" the battle is lost.

The above remarks are not made to discount the larger
fellowship of the people. Lack of awareness that there is a
connection between the various local congregations has too
often promoted the schismatic spirit as "Lone Ranger" preachers have led their congregations toward self-centered service.
A local congregation of this sort may degenerate into such an
attitude of exclusiveness that it becomes no church at all but
a veritable synagogue of Satan. The true local congregation
is also under the Lordship of Christ and is composed of members in Christ's "one body." In overlooking this point "fierce
wolves" all too often fleece "the flock" and "draw away the
disciples after them" (Acts 20:29f.).

With this concern for the house church or local congregation made clear, it may now be said that the greater number of references in the New Testament speak of the Church
as *all* the people of God in a city and its vicinity, even if they
meet in a multitude of places. This is the view found in the
very first reference to the *ekklesia* in Acts (5:11). "The
whole church" is the same as those who attended the temple
services but broke the bread of the love-feast "from house to
house" (Acts 2:46, KJV).

This "church which was in Jerusalem" was still the church
even when it was "scattered throughout the region of Judea
and Samaria," yet Paul had to enter into "house after house"
to lay "waste the church" (Acts 8:1-3). It was "the church in
Jerusalem" gathered in "house after house" or "scattered

36 CHRIST AND THE CHURCH

throughout the region." It is good that Baptists have given much attention to the "gathered church," but the "scattered church" should not be forgotten. The Church is the people of God gathered or scattered. It can be "the church throughout all Judea and Galilee" (Acts 9:31), and they can "gather together with the church" (Acts 11:26). There is "the church which meets in Jerusalem," and there is also the "church at Antioch" (Acts 11:22; 13:1).

As one continues to "run the references" this picture of the "city church," at times meeting in many places, appears again and again. It is possible that the ancient idea of the Greek city-state assembly has been incorporated into the New Testament, for the word *ekklēsia* is used precisely in this way in Acts 19:32, 39, 41. So all the people of God in a city and its vicinity constitute "a church" whether they meet in one place or many. For centuries in the history of Christianity there was never more than one church in a city even when there were thousands of members meeting in hundreds of places. It was as if one spoke of "the church of God which is in Louisville," although this church meets in more than six hundred congregations.

The view of the *ekklēsia* in Ephesians is a larger fellowship still. It is the body of Christ, the world-Church composed of all true believers, past, present, and future. Body (*sōma*) is one of two metaphors used in Ephesians 1:23 to describe the nature of the Church, the other being *plērōma* or fulness. These two great words, along with *panta*, together explain the subordination of all things to Christ.

Much has been written on the background of the body metaphor as it is used in the Pauline writings.[22] After sifting all the sources one is led back to the very first passage in the Pauline writings where the word is used specifically of Christ's body: "The cup of blessing which we bless, is it not participation in the blood of Christ? The bread which we break, is

[22] For references and a detailed discussion see Carl H. Belcher, *The Body of Christ*.

it not a participation in the body of Christ? Because there is one loaf, we who are many are one body, for we all partake of the same loaf" (I Cor. 10:16f.). As the early Pauline churches participated in "the body and blood of the Lord" (I Cor. 11:27) by eating one loaf blessed and broken in the name of the Lord Jesus, the Holy Spirit revealed to them what it means to be members of the Church: they were members of Christ's one body, the Church.

Let it here be said how important and practical the idea of the world-Church, the body of Christ, is for Christianity today. It includes all house churches in all city churches, for it is the people of God, the church militant scattered throughout the world in all ages, or gathered together as the Church triumphant at the consummation of the ages, whether in one united organization in one denomination with one standard of beliefs and practices or in many organizations with many standards of beliefs and practices and at times torn by heresy and schism. No shattered fragment can, on the basis of Scripture, justify its claim to be "the one true church" from which the rest have become separated by schism. It is painful to record, but there is "schism in the body" (I Cor. 12:25, KJV).

A modern debate is now in full swing on this point. An Anglican theologian, with the support of the New Testament, has written that the nature of the Church is such that there has often been and is now "schism in the body."[23] A "reply" has been made by a former Anglican, now a Roman Catholic and Abbott of the Benedictine monastery of Downside, near Bath, England.[24] With much in the Abbott's book one can fully agree, but not with his main thesis, which insists that there can only be "schism *from* the body," the body being the institution of the Roman Catholic Church. Pope John XXIII spoke of Protestants as "our separated brethren," but some of the sweetness of his words is dissipated when one of his influ-

---

[23] S. L. Greenslade, *Schism in the Early Church.*
[24] B. C. Butler, *The Idea of the Church.*

ential British followers can see these separated brethren only as schismatics.

The second metaphor of the Church is that of *plērōma* (fulness or fulfillment). At least three theories have been developed around the interpretation of this word. The first may be called the passive view, since it lays great stress on the *ma* ending as evidence for a passive noun, especially when it is combined with a passive participle (*plēroumenou*) interpreted as "being fulfilled" rather that as "fills." The thought of this theory may be brought out with some such translation as: "the fulfillment of him who is being fulfilled in all things in all places."

This would mean that Christ as the head of the Church is incomplete without his body the Church, but it has other implications as to the relationship between both God and Christ and the Christian and Christ. In the Colossian letter the first relationship finds expression in the statement that "all the *plērōma* of God was pleased to dwell" in Christ (1:19). If this means that God made his abode in Christ, as the analogy of Psalm 68:16 would indicate, then God is incomplete without Christ his Son. The *plērōma* dwelt in "his body of flesh" (1:22), but the *plērōma* continues to dwell in his body the Church in which the head has fulfillment and is being fulfilled.

The second relationship, that between Christ and the Christian, has found clear expression in a lofty statement about the first. "For in him the whole *plērōma* of deity dwells bodily, and you have come to fulness (*peplērōmenoi*) of life in him, who is the head of all rule and authority" (2:9f.). As the Son is "the head of all rule and authority," so is he head of all members of his body. Without these two factors the concept of the Christ is incomplete, and without the subordination of all these to him his purpose is not completed. There are no supernatural powers that have rule outside of him, so there is no place for the worship of the subordinate beings. This seems to be a major motif in Colossians 2:18f.: "Let no one disqualify you, insisting on self-abasement and worship of angels, taking his stand on visions, puffed up without reason by his sensuous mind, and not holding fast the Head, from whom the whole body, nourished and knit together through its joints and ligaments, grows with a growth that is from God."

If this view of the completion of Christ in his body the Church seems startling, it should be remembered that most of the ancient versions in Syriac, Egyptian, and Latin so translated Ephesians 1:23. Great expositors such as Origen, Theodore of Mopsuestia, Chrysostom, Calvin, and Lightfoot followed the same line.

The active view is found in the ancient versions only in the Syriac Vulgate and finds its way into the KJV, RV, ASV, RSV, etc., through Tyndale's translation of 1534. The volume in *The Tyndale New Testament Commentaries* clings still to this view, but the reasons are not compelling.[25] The passive view can care as well for 1:10, 23; 3:19; 4:10, 13; John 1:14, 16, and it is consistent with Colossians 1:24 which declares the sufferings of the head to be incomplete without the sufferings of the body, the Church.

The resultant view advanced by J. Armitage Robinson in his classic commentary comes to much the same conclusion as the passive view.[26] It may be that the passive idea should not always be pressed, but its combination with the passive participle in Ephesians 1:23, with all the ancient evidence, is difficult to discard. It seems as reasonable to interpret *plērōma* as that which is being filled as to interpret *kerygma* as that which is being preached. The body and all its members are being filled with Christ as Christ is being filled with God. The correct idea is brought out in the NEB when it renders the passage: "the church, which is his body and as such holds within it the fullness of him who himself receives the entire fullness of God."

[25] Francis Foulkes, *The Epistle of Paul to the Ephesians*, pp. 66f.
[26] *St. Paul's Epistle to the Ephesians*, pp. 42-45, 152, 255-259.

Chapter Two:

THE WORKMANSHIP OF GOD
(2:1-22)

One of the assumptions that distorts the biblical understanding of God is the unexamined idea that God once-upon-
a-time created the world and all that is in it and then became
God emeritus. He has indeed, out of his great love, created
a world subject to his care, but he did not retire after this
initial act.

A Scottish philosopher by the name of John Macmurray has
helped many, including the present writer, to recover the
biblical view of a God who continues to act in both the created
order and in human history. In one of Macmurray's most
significant writings certain statements are arresting:

> What is characteristic of the Hebrew conception of God is
> that God is primarily a worker. . . . But the religious con-
> sciousness of the Hebrew conceives God as a worker, and
> therefore, in terms of action. . . . God is actually working in
> contemporary history. . . . Here lies the crux of the whole
> matter. History is the action of God. . . . We are workers
> as God is a worker. This is our nature as human beings.[1]

All who have forgotten themselves in some labor of love
know that God is met there far more than in some retreat
from daily toil. God's Son, his obedient servant, is seen in
a new light and his voice is heard with a new power: "My
Father is working still, and I am working" (John 5:17). For
centuries this view of God has been blurred by the dominance

---

[1] John Macmurray, *The Clue to History*, pp. 33, 37, 52, 94, 99.

of Plato's Idea of the Good or of Aristotle's Unmoved Mover in Christian theology. The very idea of a God who walks in a garden and calls men to be "God's fellow workers" (I Cor. 3:15) is discounted as anthropomorphic by this aristocratic approach to the ultimate reality. Creation as the garment of the living God, and history as the arena of his action, are shoved aside and secularization triumphs.

The phrase selected as a heading for this second chapter of Ephesians is intended to give special emphasis to the belief that: "We are his workmanship, created in Christ Jesus for good works, which God prepared beforehand, that we should walk in them" (2:10). The chapter as a whole may be summarized as two great works of God in the redemption of man: the work of resurrection (2:1-10), and the work of reconciliation (2:11-22).

THE WORK OF RESURRECTION
(2:1-10)

The work of spiritual resurrection is described first as a walk of death (2:1-3) and then as a walk of life (2:4-10). It takes both to grasp the true grandeur of God's grace and man's experience of grace, which is nothing less than spiritual resurrection.

The walk of death (2:1-3). The former state of spiritual death (*ontas nekrous*) was for the Gentiles here described more than separation from God, as the human spirit is separated from the human body in physical death. It is hostile estrangement, positive resistance to the very source of spiritual life. Trespasses (*paraptōmasin*) are "false steps" that plunge men into spiritual ruin. This is more than the original sin inherited from the race; it has reference to the actual sins growing out of the inherited tendencies. It would be singular (trespass) if it were Adam's sin alone (Rom. 5:12-21). Sins (*hamartiais*) are also in the plural, for man is continuously "missing the mark" in his estrangement from God.

Before the spiritual resurrection of the Gentiles, they walked in *trespasses* and *sins*. Jewish moral laws were called *Halachah* (walking, Mk. 7:5; Acts 21:21; Heb. 13:9), and walking is a favorite moral metaphor in Ephesians. Only here and 4:17 is it used of evil conduct, for the other five times it describes proper Christian conduct (2:10; 4:1; 5:2, 8, 15). It is found at other places in the New Testament (II Cor. 5:7; Col. 4:5; I Jno. 1:6; II Jno. 4).

The pagan conduct of life among the Gentiles followed in a special way "the course of this world" and "the prince of the power of the air, the spirit that is now at work in the sons of disobedience." The first *kata* clause (*kata ton aiōna tou kosmou toutou*, "the course of this world") combines two important words. An age (*aiōn*, here translated "course") is to be understood against the background of the two great ages already mentioned in Ephesians 1:22 ("this age" and "that which is to come"), the present age being "the present evil age" (Gal. 4:4). This "present evil age" is "the age of this world" that will come to an end only at "the consummation of the ages" when the present spiritual resurrection will bear its ripe fruit in the resurrection of the body.

The world (*kosmos*) is the social system of sin which entangles and dominates all who are in estrangement from God. It is the very opposite of the fellowship (*koinonia*) created by the Holy Spirit. It is "the wisdom of this world" argued by "the debater of this age" that God has made foolish (I Cor. 1:20). It is the social system created and dominated by "the god of this age" (II Cor. 4:4, *ho theos tou aiōnas toutou*), Satan, in John called "the ruler of this world" (*ho archōn tou kosmou*, 12:31; 16:11).

Satan is "the prince of the power of the air" (*ton archonta tēs exousias tou aēros*). Many who have no difficulty in accepting the idea of "the course of this world" halt before the idea of a personal devil. Francis W. Beare no doubt speaks for many modern people when he says: "The idea of a personal devil is all but unimaginable to the mind of our own times, and is capable of interpretation only as a personification of the external forces of evil which play upon human life."[2] Yet Theodore O. Wedel, whose exposition accompanies Beare's exegesis, takes exception on the very next page with the remark: "The most modern science is growing more humble, acknowledging ignorances." Recent New Testament studies on the problem of evil would also take the "more humble" position and treat demonic powers with more recognition.[3]

Beare thinks "the course of this world" would be better translated "spirit of this world" so that "the power of the air" would be in apposition, but it is doubtful that "here alone" *aiōn* is used in the sense of later Gnostic teachers. Age seems to be a period of time; it is "the prince of the power of the air, the spirit that is now at work in the sons of disobedience" alone that is personal. The devil is not only "the god of this age" but also "the prince of the power of the air." Power (*exousia*) has reference to his authority over those alienated from God. Air (*aēr*) contrasted with the sky (*aithēr*), is the lower atmosphere, here described, to use a modern metaphor, as a spiritual belt of radiation between man and God.

From this "atmosphere" the power or spirit presses in on "the sons of disobedience." If they refuse to let God's Spirit direct their lives they become the slaves of this dominating power that is neither God nor man (Matt. 12: 22-45; Mk. 3:22-27; Lk. 11:4-26; 22:3; Jno. 13:2, 27; Acts 5:3). This personal power that oppresses man is now at work (*nun energountos*), and the only power adequate to undo and destroy his work is the working God whose workmanship is all in Christ (cf. 1:11, 20). In the obedient, God is at work, but they are opposed in the social and spiritual struggle by Satan and "the sons of disobedience." On the obedient, God bestows his grace, but "the wrath of God comes upon the sons of disobedience" (Eph. 5:6).

Thus far the world and the devil, the social and spiritual

[2] *The Interpreter's Bible*, Vol. 10, p. 639.
[3] G. B. Caird, *Principalities and Powers;* Heinrich Schlier, *Principalities and Powers in the New Testament.*

powers of death, have been discussed in relation to the Gentiles. It must not be assumed that Jews were not so involved, as Ephesians 2:3 is careful to say: "Among these we also once lived in the passions of our flesh, following the desires of body and mind, and so we were by nature children of wrath like the rest of mankind" (cf. Rom. 2:1-9; 3:9, 23). Three powers dominate all who have not the grace of God in Christ: the social power of the world, the spiritual power of the devil, and the sensual power of the flesh.

The sensual "passions" (*epithumiai*) describe the eager desire with which one indulges in sin. They are more psychological than physical, although the physical organism becomes the instrument of such desires. Even the term "flesh" (*sarx*) is more psychological than physical, for it describes man's life organized around himself rather than God (cf. Gal. 5:16-21; Rom. 8:4-9).

The physical and psychological factors are strongly suggested in the phrase "desires of the flesh and mind" (*thelēmata tēs sarkos kai tōn dianoiōn*). *Thelēmata* means literally "the wills" or "the wishes" of the mind. *Dianoia* (mind) means the process of reasoning that involves the intellect, so that passions and desires are never completely blind and irrational (cf. Col. 1:21). The reason becomes dominated by eager longing and desire and all discretion is thrown to the wind.

This social, spiritual, sensual system makes men "children of wrath." God's original intention in creation and his ultimate will in redemption is to bestow on them his love, but in this state of spiritual death men experience *orgē* (wrath) when they should experience *agapē* (love). Wrath is God's love spurned by disobedient men who refuse to love God and man in obedience to God.

Sin, according to the distinctive view in Scripture, involves a close relation between pride and pleasure, self-love and sensuality. It is "defilement of body and spirit" (II Cor. 7:1). With a different terminology Augustine classified sins as carnalities and animosities, sins of the flesh and sins of the soul.[4] In one of his most penetrating statements he says: "It was not the corruptible flesh that made the soul corrupt, but the sinful soul that made the flesh corruptible."[5]

It is unfortunate that Augustine's penetrating insight into the empirical nature of sin became confused by a theory of inherited guilt. In his conflict with the Pelagians he always assumes that original sin is original guilt, and on this his dismal view of total depravity draws the conclusion that infants, whose guilt is not removed by baptism, are damned, even though with a milder punishment than the wicked (*De Baptismo Parvulorum*, I. 20). One illustration assumes that twins, exposed by a harlot at birth, were separated, one in hell and the other in heaven, simply because some merciful person baptized one (*Contra Julianum*, II. 14). Another illustration does not question the notion that the unbaptized infant of a pious woman is damned, while the baptized infant of an enemy of Christ is saved (*Contra Julianum*, II. 11). *Phusei* (by nature) has reference to habitual action, as in Romans 2:14. It does not exclude original sin as an innate tendency by birth, for *phusei* is so used in Galatians 2:15 (cf. Rom. 2:27; 9:24), but the idea of original or inherited guilt is to be rejected. It is a disastrous doctrine that has done untold damage and distorted the doctrine of baptism until this day.

Corporate sin, or original sin inherited as a tendency by the race, is described in the hymn of Adam and Christ in Romans 5:12-21, but Ephesians 2:1-3 is concerned more with actual sin as set forth with equal detail in Romans 1:18-32. Sins are classified as ungodliness and unrighteousness. Ungodliness (1:18-25) is the ignorance that darkens the mind of rebellious men (1:18-23) and the idolatry that fills the place of God with some substitute (1:24f.). Unrighteousness (1:26-32) includes both the sins of the human flesh, carnalities, such as homosexuality (1:26f.), and the many sins of the human spirit (1:28-32).

[4] *City of God,* XIV. 2.
[5] *Ibid.,* XIV. 3.

The radical realism of Reinhold Niebuhr has done much to restore the biblical understanding of sin to the theology of the last generation. His penetrating analysis of sin as self-love out of which the various forms of sensuality grow as escapes from frustrations is a needed corrective to the Puritanism that is all too often preoccupied with "sinful pleasure" to the neglect of gross self-righteousness.

In the ancient baptismal liturgies, it was this realistic view of sin that made the words of renunciation so solemn and fearful.[6] The devil with all his pomp and works was renounced as the catechumens faced the West, the symbol of darkness, and then they turned to the East, the symbol of light, to give the words of adherence to Christ. "A *pompa* was, in the culture of antiquity, a festive procession, a triumphal procession, a marching around some god's feast, at which all idols were carried along. The devil is, as it were, constantly conducting such triumphal procession in the world; all who serve the devil and live in sin are running along in this procession. But in baptism the candidate drops out of this procession, he leaves the devil's camp, and enters into the camp of Christ's army."[7] In baptism, the normal form of which was immersion, the candidate descended into the water by three steps, and these three steps (in some sections at least) symbolized his renunciation. Hildephonsus of Toledo, Spain, says: "Three as you go down for the three at which renunciation is made, that is, at which the devil is renounced, and his angels and his works and his commands."[8]

The walk of life (2:4-10). Against this dark background of death the grace of God does indeed turn man to the light. Both Jews and Gentiles ("us," "you") owe the new life to the act and gift of God: "But God who is rich in mercy, out of the great love with which he loved us." Out of the fountain of love flows the richness of God's mercy. Mercy calls at-

---

[6] E. C. Whitaker, *Documents of the Baptismal Liturgies*, pp. 5, 25, 29, 43, 100, 121, 201, 205.

[7] Joseph A. Jungmann, *The Early Liturgy*, p. 80.

[8] Whitaker, *op. cit.*, p. 104.

tention to the pitiful plight of man before the compassion of God, and love points to the profound depths of God out of which all mercy flows.

Twice the searchlight of love sweeps the scope of God's grace past, present, and future. In the first sweep it is God's act that appears: "But God . . . when we were dead through our trespasses, made us alive together with Christ (by grace you have been saved), and raised us up with him, and made us sit with him in the heavenly places in Christ Jesus, that in the coming ages he might show the immeasurable riches of his grace in kindness in Christ Jesus" (2:5-7). In the past, when we were in the condition of death, he "made us alive." This making alive was proclaimed in Christian baptism (Col. 2:11-14; Rom. 6:1-11), the ethical implications of which are described in Colossians 3:1-17 as a putting to death (5-11) of the old practices overcome in Christ and a putting on (12-17) of the things that make a portrait of Christ. In a very real way, as portrayed in baptism, we are "made alive together with Christ" (cf. "in" and "with" in Col. 2:9-13).

In the present he who "raised us up with him" has also "made us sit with him in the heavenly places in Christ Jesus" (2:6). The posture of sitting is one of the three used to describe the Christian conduct. Walking is the most prominent and has reference to daily behavior. Standing comes up later as the posture of a Christian in opposition to sin (Eph. 6:11). The sitting here described is a picture of life lived "in the heavenly places in Christ." It is possible to be in "the heavenly place," the spiritual realm, and not be "in Christ Jesus," as in the case of demonic powers (3:10; 6:12), but it is not possible to be "in Christ Jesus" and not be "in the heavenly places." Here and now heaven has come down to kiss earth in the experience of grace (1:3).

As God raised Christ "from the dead and made him sit at his right hand in the heavenly places" (1:20), so has "he raised us up with him in the heavenly places in Christ Jesus" (2:6). It is this that is repeatedly portrayed each time baptism is rightly performed. The mode of baptism is rooted in the meaning, and Martin Luther is surely correct when he insists on the mode of immersion on the basis of both language and meaning: "This usage is also demanded by the significance of baptism, for baptism signifies that the old man and the sinful birth of flesh and blood are to be wholly drowned by the grace of God, as we shall hear. We should, therefore, do justice to its meaning and make baptism a true and complete sign of the thing signified."[9]

This present act of God that raises up man is in order to perform a future act: "that in the coming ages he might show the immeasurable riches of his grace in kindness in Christ Jesus" (2:7). The "coming ages" perhaps mean the same as "the fulness of times" when, in Christ, God will "unite things in him, things in heaven, and things on earth" (1:10). Even now the unity in the Church, the body of Christ, is a foretaste, meager as it is in the modern world, of this future harvest of the mighty act of God.

Eternity, as taught in the Bible, is no static situation where no distinctions are made.[10] The Bible does not picture God as some Idea of the Good or Unmoved Mover, to whom past, present, and future have no meaning. Yet this "night in which all cows are black" is constantly being confused with the biblical view of eternity. It is profoundly true to say of God "from everlasting to everlasting thou art God" (Ps. 90:2), but this does not mean that he is indifferent to and unconscious of time. "The steadfast love of the LORD is from everlasting to everlasting, upon those who fear him, and his righteousness to children's children" (Ps. 103:17). This is no timeless picture. History is God's act and it is preserved in eternity. The Greek phrases "unto the ages of the ages" (Phil. 4:20) and "unto all the ages" (Jude 25) mean the same.

This act of God is a gift (Eph. 2:8-10). The idea so pos-

---

[9] *Treatise on Baptism*, I.
[10] This has been profoundly refuted by Oscar Cullmann, *Christ and Time*.

sesses the author that it was dropped into the middle of the sentence at 2:5 ("by grace you have been saved"). Now it is taken up afresh for elaboration and explanation: "For by grace you have been saved through faith; and this is not your own doing, it is the gift of God — not because of works, lest any man should boast" (2:8f.). The relationship between grace and faith has been distorted in the theologies of Augustine and Calvin and the systems based on their thought. Starting with the total depravity of man, faith has been interpreted as irresistible and the gift of God to man. The result is the double decree by which God gives some men faith and the rest are left in their sins (Augustine) or predestined to hell (Calvin).

Much has been made of this passage, because it is one of the few New Testament passages that can be so distorted. It is God's saving act that is the gift of God, not faith. Faith is man's acceptance of this gift freely given. The Greek will not sustain the idea that faith is God's gift. A. T. Robertson has clearly interpreted the passage: "'Grace' is God's part, 'faith' ours. And that (*kai touto*). Neuter, not feminine *tautē* and so refers not to *pistis* (feminine) or to *charis* (feminine also), but to the act of being saved by grace conditioned on faith on our part."[11]

No other passage in the New Testament can be called in to support the doctrine of a double decree executed by irresistible grace. Galatians 5:22 speaks of *pistis* as the fruit of the Spirit, but this is faithfulness after one has believed and received the Spirit. Second Corinthians 4:13 has much the same idea in mind when it speaks of "the same spirit of faith." Romans 12:3 mentions "the measure of faith which God assigned," but this is living faith, not the initial faith by which one enters the process of salvation. First Timothy 1:14 says "the grace of our Lord overflowed for me with the faith and love that are in Christ Jesus," but this is no picture

---

[11] *Word Pictures in the New Testament*, IV (1931), 525.

of an irresistible power that selects one and rejects another. The latter is the nearest passage in the New Testament to the Augustinian thory, especially when reference is made to "those who were to believe for eternal life" (I Tim. 1:16), but even here one can make shipwreck of faith (I Tim. 1:19). This seems always the picture in the New Testament.

Salvation is a perfect state: "you have been saved." This does not rule out salvation as a process. We have indeed "been saved," but we are also "being saved" (I Cor. 1:18) in the present, and "we will be saved" (Rom. 5:9) in the future salvation which "is nearer to us now than when we first believed" (Rom. 13:11). To interpret this as "realized eschatology," as if there was no future perspective, is to overlook the future redemption clearly taught in the Ephesian letter (1:14; 4:30). The present is a wonderful foretaste of the future, but it is not the future.

To this discussion of the relationship between grace and faith should be added some remarks on the relationship between grace and good works (cf. Gal. 2:16; Rom. 3:20, 28; 4:1-5; II Tim. 1:9, Tit. 3:5). We are not saved by works, "lest any man should boast," but we are saved for good works that grow out of the experience of grace. Salvation by works would only increase the pride and self-righteousness that are the very root of all sin (cf. Gal. 6:14), but the religious life that does not produce good works is based on a superficial faith.

Good works and grace go together in the miracle of a transformed life. "For we are his workmanship, created in Christ Jesus for good works, which God prepared beforehand, that we should walk in them" (Eph. 2:10). Workmanship (*poiēma*) is a word found in the New Testament only here and in Romans 1:20 ("in the things that have been made"), but it is the result of the work of God's grace in Christ. Our word "poem," a metrical composition, comes from this Greek word. This work is the beginning of the new creation in Christ (2:15; 4:24; II Cor. 5:17). God has predestined good works for those in Christ, and his election always includes service as well as salvation (Tit. 2:14).

God is a Creator, and his workmanship among men is a new creation. Legalism and ceremonialism are seen as a form of spiritual bondage, "for neither circumcision counts for anything, nor uncircumcision, but a new creation" (Gal. 6:15). The God who rolled back the darkness with his light in creation has shined forth into the darkness of the human heart (II Cor. 4:6). "Therefore, if any one is in Christ, he is a new creation; the old has passed away, behold, the new has come" (II Cor. 5:17). Man is created anew for a new morality (Col. 3:10; Eph. 4:24).

The Work of Reconciliation
(2:11-22)

A second way to describe the redemptive work of God in Christ is to use the concept of *reconciliation*. Spiritual resurrection is set against the dark background of spiritual death, but reconciliation works against the barrier of hostility toward both God and man. This is depicted in three steps: separation from God (2:11f.), reconciliation to God (2:12-18), and the habitation of God (2:19-22).

Separation from God (2:11f.). The separation of the Gentiles from God is indicated both by a physical sign and a spiritual state. The physical sign was uncircumcision: "Therefore remember that at one time you Gentiles in the flesh, called the uncircumcision by what is called the circumcision, which is made in the flesh by hands" (2:11). Physical circumcision was made in the flesh by human hands, and this was the boast of the Jews and the sign of their superior privilege over the Gentiles. "You Gentiles in the flesh," from the Jewish perspective, summed up their sign of separation from God.

In contrast to this literal circumcision is a very different spiritual circumcision. "For in Christ Jesus neither circumcision nor uncircumcision is of any avail, but faith working through love" (Gal. 5:6). "For neither circumcision counts for anything, nor uncircumcision, but a new creation" (Gal. 6:15). "In him also you were circumcised with a circumcision made without hands, by putting off the body of flesh in the circumcision of Christ; and you were buried with him in baptism, in which you were also raised with him through faith in the working of God, who raised him from the dead" (Col. 2:11f.). In summary: "For he is not a real Jew who is one outwardly, nor is true circumcision something external and physical. He is a Jew who is one inwardly and real circumcision is a matter of the heart, spiritual and not literal. His praise is not from men but from God" (Rom. 2:28f.). A word that was once a sign of superiority and pride has, by the work of God's grace through faith, been transformed to mean true inwardness and humility.

The spiritual state of the Gentiles before they received the circumcision of Christ in believer's baptism corresponds with their physical sign: "Remember that you were at that time separated from Christ, alienated from the commonwealth of Israel, and strangers to the covenants of promise, having no hope and without God in the world" (2:12).

Separation from Christ deprived the Gentiles of "every spiritual blessing in the heavenly places" (Eph. 1:3). Union with Christ gave them a share in these blessings now and "in the coming ages" (Eph. 2:7). They are united with him in whom God intends "to unite all things" (Eph. 1:11). This ultimate union of all things has already begun the union of Jews and Gentiles in the one body of Christ, the Church. The rift of race and religious rite has been removed. A comment by Canon Wedel should shatter the false security of many modern Christians: "If we are ever puzzled as to why Mohammedanism and Communism (there are similarities between them) are such stubborn rivals to Christianity, one explanation may be discovered in the fact that in both racial disunity has been abolished."[12]

---

[12] *The Interpreter's Bible*, Vol. 10, p. 650.

Alienation from the commonwealth of Israel excluded the Gentiles from the holy nation that God had chosen as his own people. "And you, who once were estranged and hostile in mind, doing evil deeds, he has now reconciled in his body of flesh by his death, in order to present you holy and blameless and irreproachable before him, provided that you continue in the faith, stable and steadfast, not shifting from the hope of the gospel which you heard, which has been preached to every creature under heaven, and of which I, Paul, became a minister" (Col. 1:21-23). In Christ even Gentiles have become the people of God (I Pet. 2:9f.).

As "strangers to the covenants of promise," the Gentiles had seen the stream of salvation history flow far from their fields. In a spiritual desert there was no promise of a future harvest. Covenants with the Patriarchs (Gen. 15:8-21; 17:1-21) and with the nation under Moses (Ex. 24:1-11) had not brought the harvest of a holy nation, but the hope of a new covenant had been kept alive by prophetic promise (Jer. 31:31-34; 32:40; Isa. 55:3; Ezek. 37:26).

As Gentiles they had no such hope. For Greeks the golden age was in the past. Without God there is no real hope in this life or in the life to come. Hope that is poorly founded and confined to this life is a miserable thing (I Cor. 15:19). Even death does not destroy the Christian hope (I Thess. 4:13). A hymn of hope in Titus 2:11-14 is a splendid summary of this eternal theme. It is beautifully translated by Helen Barrett Montgomery in the Centenary Translation:

> For God's grace has shined forth
> Bringing salvation to all men
> And schooling us to renounce impiety and evil passions,
> And to live soberly, righteously, and godly in this present age;
>
> While we look for the blessed hope and epiphany
> Of the glory of our great God and Saviour, Jesus Christ.
> He gave himself for us to redeem us from all iniquity,
> And to purify unto himself a people zealous of good works.

The total condition of the Gentiles is described as *atheoi* (without God), from which we get the word "atheists." They were not atheists in the modern sense, however, for they believed in many gods (Gal. 4:8; I Cor. 8:4). They were without hope in the true and living God who has revealed himself in Christ Jesus our Lord.

The practical atheism of the present, in which pleasures and possessions often constitute all the security of social groups, is not unlike the pessimism of the pagan world. The fanaticism with which many cling to material things can only signify that things are their god.

Reconciliation to God (2:13-18). Isaiah 57:19 had promised: "Peace, peace, to the far off and to the near." Paul now proclaims that this has come to pass: "But now in Christ Jesus you who once were far off have been brought near in the blood of Christ" (2:13). William Barclay, following Abbott, mentions a Rabbinic story of a Gentile woman who confessed to Rabbi Eliezer that she was a sinner and begged him thus: "Rabbi, bring me near." The Rabbi refused, and the door was shut in her face. The Christ of the cross shuts the door in no faces, be they Gentile, woman, or any other sinner. The blood of Christ has opened the way to the universal "now" (*nuni*) that invites the Jews and Gentiles alike to accept the peace that God offers. This peace is one of the most precious words to describe the reconciliation of man to God. In 2:14-18 this peace is expounded in a threefold way.

There is first the prince of peace (2:14). Isaiah 9:6f. promised a "Prince of Peace" in whom "the increase of his government and of peace there will be no end" (cf. Mic. 5:5; Isa. 53:5; Hag. 2:9; Zech. 9:10; Lk. 2:14). Now Christ is declared to be "our peace, who has made us both one, and has broken down the dividing wall of hostility" (2:14). The barrier of the wall called forth a vivid picture known by Jews and Gentiles alike. Josephus describes the wall as follows: "Proceeding across this toward the second court of the temple, one found it surrounded by a stone balustrade, three cubits high and of exquisite workmanship; in this at regular intervals stood slabs giving warning, some in Greek,

others in Latin characters, of the law of purification, to wit,
that no foreigner was permitted to enter the holy place, for
so the second enclosure of the temple was called" (*Jewish
War*, V.v.2, Loeb; cf. VI.2.4). In the *Antiquities of the Jews*
(15.11.5, Whiston) he describes the wall further: "This was
encompassed by a stone wall for a partition, with an in-
scription which forbade any foreigner to go in under pain of
death." Two of these inscriptions have been discovered, one
in 1871 and another in 1935. The one discovered by the
French archaeologist M. Clermont Ganneau in 1871, written
in Greek, now in Constantinople, says: "No man of another
race is to proceed within the partition and enclosing wall
about the sanctuary; and anyone arrested there will have himself to blame for the penalty of death which will be imposed
as a consequence."

The breaking of the wall took place long before the destruction of the temple, in A.D. 70. The wall between the
Court of the Gentiles and the Court of the Women symbolized
the racial and religious hostility that made the Gentiles an
"out group." Even the women were an "out group" to some
degree, for they were not allowed to go into the other three
courts: the Court of the Israelites, the Court of the Priests,
and the Holy Place itself. Paul knew all this, and he was
arrested because of the rumor that he had taken Trophimus
beyond the barrier (Acts 21:28f.). In the cross of Christ all
groups become "in groups." Christ excludes none, for racial
and religious hostility are removed by the reconciling act
of his death.

Then there is the price of peace (2:15f.; cf. II Cor. 5:18-
20; Rom. 5:10; Col. 1:22). There is first the abolition (*katar-
gēsas*) of "the law of commandments and ordinances" described with such vigor in Galatians (cf. Col. 2:14, 20).
Romans 10:4 has summarized the situation: "For Christ is the
end of the law, that every one who has faith may be justified."

The abolition makes reconciliation possible. He "abolished
in his flesh the law of commandments and ordinances, that

he might create in himself one new man in place of the two,
so making peace, and might reconcile us both to God in one
body through the cross, thereby bringing hostility to an
end" (2:15f.). This "one new man" is the "one body." The
new man (*kainos anthropos*) is a new kind of man, a man new
in quality. Another Greek word, *neos*, means quantitative
newness. Thousands of the same type could have existed before, as is suggested by the name Neapolis (New City), the
port for Philippi. But this new man is *qualitatively* new
(*kainos*), for there is no other like him. God broke the
mold when he was made. There has never been and there
will never be another like him, for there is only one body of
Christ.

The "one body" which is the "one new man" is the Christian
fellowship. How can people who profess to believe that the
New Testament is our only rule of faith and order fail to see
this unmistakable teaching? (I Cor. 10:17; 12:12f.; Col. 1:18,
24; 2:17, 19; 3:15; Eph. 1:23; 2:16; 3:6; 4:4, 12, 16; 5:23, 30;
Rom. 12:5.) It is no wonder that the cross through which the
reconciliation has been accomplished has been replaced as a
symbol on our churches by a weathervane. Could it be that
the churches really are more concerned with which way the
wind is blowing than with bearing the cross of Christ, in a
world of racial and religious hostility?

Those who confess that there is one body in Christ have the
greatest faith and the greatest fellowship this side of heaven.
It is a state of heaven. When we are truly this "one new man"
in this body," it may truly be said in the translation by J. B.
Phillips: "now the war is over" (2:16). But alas, many, even
many who profess to follow Christ, do not yet know "the war
is over," that racial and religious hostility has ended.

We need also the preaching of peace (2:17f.). We have the
access (*prosagōgē*) opened to all, both Jews and Gentiles. The
prosagōgeus at the Persian court introduced the people to the
king, and it is Christ who introduces us to God, who leads us
out of our hostility into the peace of God's presence. In the
"one body" there is only "one Spirit." Outside the "one body"

one cannot have the "one Spirit," and without the "one Spirit" one is not a member of the "one body." "For by one Spirit we were all baptized into one body—Jews or Greeks, slaves or free—and all were made to drink of one Spirit" (I Cor. 12: 13). That one body exists now, for one cannot be baptized into a body that does not yet exist.

We have the access, but we need the accent. We need to proclaim what Christ proclaimed, to evangelize as he evangelized (euēggelisato). If we do not evangelize we will fossilize, and God's chosen people will indeed become God's frozen people. Jesus came to fulfil Isaiah 57:19, for "he came to preach peace to you who are far off and peace to those who were near; for through him we both have access in one Spirit to the Father" (2:17f.). It is our responsibility to accent the access with the prayer that others will accept.

Ephesians 2:13-18 holds the solution to some of the bitter racial and religious hostilities of our time. These words were written in a world where Jews called all who were not of their race "Gentiles"; Greeks called all who did not speak the Greek language and share the Greek culture "barbarians." The word "barbarian" is derived from the opinion that those who did not speak their language merely babbled ("bar bar") instead of speaking intelligibly. Romans looked on all others as pagans; masters looked upon slaves and males looked upon females as property. It is difficult for us to realize how revolutionary are the words: "There is neither Jew nor Greek, there is neither slave nor free; for you are all one in Christ Jesus" (Gal. 3: 28). Or again: "Here there cannot be Greek and Jew, circumcised and uncircumcised, barbarian, Scythian, slave, free man, but Christ is all, and in all" (Col. 3:11).

The problem of Jewish-Gentile relation was a burning issue in the early Church. Even the apostolic mission was complicated by the question, as the controversy over circumcision indicates. Jewish Christians, clinging to the proselyte practice which required circumcision before baptism, were deeply disturbed when Paul altered the custom and received them by faith and baptism without circumcision. Not even the agreement that the apostleship to the circumcision would be the mission of Peter and those associated with him and that the apostleship of the uncircumcision would be left to Paul, settled the situation (Gal. 2:6-10).

The tension called for a long discussion when the majority of Jewish people did not embrace the belief in Jesus as the Christ, and the eschatological hope of Paul was profoundly influenced by the problem. His solution was found in the hope that after the full number of the Gentiles was reached, all Israel would be saved (Rom. 11:25f.) and the purpose of God for the nations would be finally fulfilled. Some have drawn the conclusion on this basis that Paul was a univeralist, but it is more likely that this had reference to a universal mission which offered opportunity to Gentiles and Jews alike.[13]

A partial solution to the issue for both circumcision and the consummation, in both ecclesiology and eschatology, is found in the concept of the one body of Christ in which the Jewish man and the Gentile man are made one new man in the cross of Christ (Eph. 2:14). At the cross the eschatological hope is partly realized already, but this does not remove the prospects of a perfect solution at the *parousia*.

Neglect of the New Testament teachings on this problem has left a history of anti-Semitism that is a shameful blotch on church history. In the nineteenth century beginning in America the freedom granted to Jewish people often led to unusual conversions to the Christian faith, and this is a chapter in the history of the Church that should not be forgotten.[14] Unfortunately it was all but forgotten by some New Testament scholars in the Nazi regime. Gerhard Kittel, editor of the famous Greek dictionary (*Wörterbuch*), greatly compromised himself by supporting a suggestion that Jewish Christians and Gentile Christians should have separate con-

[13] More discussion on this point may be found in my forthcoming book *The Hope of Glory*, Ch. 6.
[14] It is told well by Jakob Jocz, *The Jewish People and Jesus Christ* pp. 201-261.

gregations and that in no case should a non-Jewish congregation have a Jewish minister.[15]

> *In Christ there is no East or West,*
> *In Him no South or North;*
> *But one great fellowship of love*
> *Throughout the whole wide earth.*
>
> *In Him shall true hearts everywhere*
> *Their high communion find;*
> *His service is the golden cord,*
> *Close binding all mankind.*
>
> *Join hands, then, brothers of the faith,*
> *Whatever your race may be:*
> *Who serves my Father as a son*
> *Is surely kin to me.*
>
> *In Christ now meet both East and West,*
> *In Him meet South and North:*
> *And Christly souls are one in Him,*
> *Throughout the whole wide earth.*

Habitation with God (2:19-22). It has always been God's
intention to dwell among his people. The garden, the many
holy places, the temple in the Old Testament, all bear witness
to this belief. Some speculation has raised the question
whether the incarnation of Christ and his continuing indwelling in the Church would have taken place had there been no
fall into sin and the need of the reconciling cross. Even
though this does focus attention on God's eternal intention
to dwell among his people, the answer to such a question is
impossible. Of one thing we may be sure, namely that sin
does not finally defeat God's plan to indwell his people that
they may dwell in him. The removal of sin by reconciliation
makes way for the habitation of God with his own.

At this point the *physiological* metaphor of the body is
enriched with the *political* metaphor of a commonwealth and

---

[15] The sad story is told in its best light by J. R. Porter, "The Case
of Gerhard Kittel," *Theology*, L (1947), 401-406.

the *architectural* metaphor of a temple.[16] The Church is a city in which Gentiles are "no longer strangers and sojourners" but "fellow citizens with the saints and members of the household of God" (2:19). The concept of a commonwealth as a historical community has as its background "the commonwealth of Israel" (2:12), an idea that once excluded the Gentiles. Now the concept includes Jews and Gentiles, for the cross of Christ has made them one people, a new humanity. As strangers (*xenoi*) the Gentiles had no political rights, and as sojourners (*paroikoi*) they were only temporary residents.

More than once the concept of the Church as the city of God has sustained faith in the midst of crumbling civilization. The most celebrated example took place soon after the first collapse of ancient Rome in A.D. 410 when Alaric and his Goths plunged the civilized world into despair. Three years later, in A.D. 413, a North African bishop sat down to write *The City of God*, a book that was to nurture the faith of millions for centuries. Over a period of thirteen years Augustine of Hippo pondered the differences between the early city of this world and the eternal city of God. At the end of his most important book in the work, with a flash of genuine insight, he summed things up: "Accordingly, two cities have been formed by two loves: the earthly by the love of self, even to the contempt of God; the heavenly by the love of God, even to the contempt of self. The former, in a word, glories in itself, the latter in the Lord" (XIV. 28).

This city of God is also the household (*oikeioi*) of God, for there all men are "kinsmen." The *xenoi* (strangers) and *paroikoi* (sojourners) have become *oikeioi* (kinsmen) in the one family of God. Clans such as "the house of David" and "the house of Hapsburg" pass away, but "the house of God" goes on forever.

It is this concept of "the household of God" that has been so clearly grasped by Lesslie Newbigin in his book by that

---

[16] *The Interpreter's Bible*, Vol. 10, pp. 660f.

title.[17] Newbigin excludes none of God's children in assessing the different groups of Christians. Catholics have retained the New Testament teaching on the one body of Christ even if they identify it too closely with one ecclesiastical institution. The Protestant return to justification by faith stirred the reform of ecclesiastical traditions in the light of Holy Scripture, even if this did at times degenerate into a sterile orthodoxy. To these two types he rightly adds the Pentecostal, which has attempted the recovery of fellowship created by the Holy Spirit. When "the household of God" is set in order all of these elements will have their proper place and proportion.

The architectural metaphor of the temple grows logically out of the political metaphor, for the household of God is "built upon the foundation of the apostles and prophets, Christ Jesus himself being the chief cornerstone, in whom the whole structure is joined together and grows into a holy temple in the Lord" (2:20f.).

First Corinthians 3:10-15 speaks of a building, the church, of which Christ is the foundation, and Christians are the materials used in the construction. A similar picture is found in I Peter 2:4-8. In Ephesians 2:20 Christ is the cornerstone (akrogōniaos), the stone at the summit that completes the building. The apostles and prophets are the foundation and Christ is the copestone. It will later be seen (3:5; 4:11) that these apostles are not the Twelve but more like the modern missionaries (cf. Acts 14:14; Rom. 16:7; I Cor. 12:28f.; II Cor. 8:23). Likewise, the prophets are not those of the Old Testament but those of the New Testament (Acts 13:1; 21:10; I Cor. 12:28f.; 14:29, 32, 37). The Didache has specific regulations for these traveling teachers that planted the Church in new places, a type of "pioneer missionaries" (XI-XIII).

As the metaphor of a building moves forward it merges with that of the body. In Christ "each several building, fitly framed together groweth into a holy temple in the Lord" (2:21, ASV). The Greek phrase pasa oikodomē does not mean "all the build-

17 See Bibliography.

ing" (KJV) or " the whole structure" (RSV). One can never be dogmatic on such a fine point, but it is perhaps correct to view "every building" (ASV fn.) as a local congregation, the house church or city church, that is joined to other local congregations to make the one temple of the Lord, the one body of Christ. In Christ local congregations are interdependent, because they are all "in Christ" (Gal. 1:22, ASV). This is the basis for all true "cooperation" and "association." When this is neglected, "lone rangers" lead the flock astray (Acts 20:28-30) and united effort is made difficult. A true congregation "is joined together" with other congregations and "grows into a holy temple in the Lord."

The temple (*naos*) is literally a sanctuary. It is not the priestly edifice (*hieron*), as in I Corinthians 9:13, but the inner sanctuary, the *naos hagios*. The growth of the temple is the same as the growth of the body, and both belong to the Lord, the copestone of the temple and the head of the body.

It has well been said that the modern Church suffers acutely from an "edifice complex." Too often we forget that the great medieval cathedrals and parish churches were no part of primitive Christianity. For three hundred years, until the era of Constantine the Great, Christians worshipped in catacombs, houses, and at best in a converted synagogue. The Church was the people of God, and edifices were only meeting places. The places were much more like a Quaker meetinghouse or a Brethren hall than the medieval and modern buildings that are all too often not the "meeting place" of the multitudes. Perhaps the Church has not learned well: "The Lord who made the world and everything in it, being Lord of heaven and earth, does not live in shrines made by man" (Acts 17: 24).

Growing and building go together, for the body is the building. The building that began at one point (aorist tense, 2:20) passes through a process of being built (present tense, 2:22) that has now reached across the centuries. No temple made with human hands, however beautiful and symbolic, can compare with that which is made of all the redeemed souls of salvation history. With this faith and hope, the Church separates from the world to make visible the true temple of God here and now (II Cor. 6:14-7:1). She is no invisible temple, for she is made of humble people who walk with God in many different places until they find rest at the end of the way.

Chapter Three:

THE WISDOM OF GOD
(3:1-21)

Making known God's manifold wisdom is God's cosmic purpose in the Church. If God's plan of the ages is forgotten and secondary concerns suck away the vitality of the Christian witness, the Church becomes more concerned with her own comfort than with confronting the world with Christ. Modern Christianity has rightly magnified missions as the main task to which Christians should devote their energies, but there is an increasing danger that recession has set in.

It was this type of recession that made the most majestic monument to the wisdom of God a present tragic symbol. *Hagia Sophia* (Holy Wisdom) in Constantinople, monument of the Emperor Justinian in the sixth century, and one of the most beautiful buildings on earth, is today a secular museum. It is a silent reminder that a once great Christian culture may crumble and leave the people in desperate need of spiritual renewal.

One of the Orthodox theologians who has made a considerable contribution to renewal of thought and stimulated some action in politics and education interprets *Hagia Sophia* in a way that recovers some of the missionary vision of the original New Testament concept. In summary of the symbolism he says: "An ocean of light pours in from above and dominates the whole space below — it enchants, convinces, as it seems to say: I am in the world and the world is in me."[1]

[1] Sergius Bulgakov, *The Wisdom of God*, p. 13.

Perhaps a careful consideration of the major ideas of this chapter, focused around the idea of the wisdom of God (3:10), will help to correct this distorted notion of Christian unity. Real Christian unity takes place and grows when people gather together for corporate worship and witness, not when prelates plan in an ivory tower the things they think good for "the people." God's wisdom is stated as the purpose of God (3:1-13) and the power of God (3:14-21). A surrender of either of the two foci is fatal for the life of the church, for one is witness and the other is worship.

THE PURPOSE OF GOD
(3:1-13)

The purpose of God was made known to "the prisoner of Christ Jesus in behalf of you Gentiles" (3:1). Paul does speak of himself as "a prisoner of Christ Jesus" (Philemon 1, 9) but here the article (*ho desmios, the* prisoner) is intended to accentuate his special mission to the Gentiles. It is not so much the Romans who have taken him prisoner but "Christ Jesus," the one anointed of God for the fulfilment of his purpose (Acts 10:38). Paul has been captured by Christ to continue this plan and purpose.

Paul is to accomplish God's purpose among "the Gentiles," as Peter was assigned the mission to the Jews. One of the most decisive events in salvation history took place when this twofold mission became clear to the Jerusalem "pillars" (Gal. 2:1-10), and much misunderstanding of the New Testament follows when this is forgotten.[2] The emphatic phrase "you, the Gentiles" (*humōn tōn ethnōn,* cf. 2:11 *humeis ta ethnē*), includes all Gentiles in all places. The Gentile world is Paul's parish, and he is preaching to them from his prison pulpit. To the Colossians he said: "Now I rejoice in my sufferings for your sake, and in my flesh I complete what is lacking in Christ's afflictions for the sake of his body, that is the church"

[2] This is discussed in detail in my forthcoming book *The Hope of Glory,* ch. 5.

(1:24), and even there his focus is on "the Gentiles" (1:27). He builds the body with Gentiles while Peter builds it with Jews, but there is only one body, not two (2:14-18).

At this point the sentence is broken by a parenthesis that separates the subject from the verb by twelve verses (2-13). Codex Bezae and Ambroiaster (Hilary) insert the verb *presbeuō* ("I am ambassador") to simplify the sentence, but the real verb in the best text is *kamptō* ("I bow," 3:14). While Paul waits to bow his knees a stream flows from this mouth that floods the mind with a world vision of the purpose of God. Out of the vast enigma of the divine mystery is unveiled the purpose of God in Paul and in the church. The purpose includes the revelation (3:1-6). and the proclamation of God's mystery (3:7-13).

The revelation of the mystery (3:1-6). This revelation is described around three significant words, each of which must be given special attention. The first word is *oikonomia* (stewardship): "assuming that you have heard of the stewardship of God's grace that was given to me for you." The translation of *oikonomia* as "dispensation" in the King James Version was meaningful in 1611 when dispensation had reference to dealing out and management, but it is inadequate today. The misunderstanding of the word has been complicated by the system of seven dispensations made popular in the *Scofield Reference Bible*, a Bible that has some helpful notes at other places but not here.

Oikonomia has reference to God's management of his household, and a part of this management was the giving of the gospel of grace to Paul so that he could distribute it to the Gentiles. He had said in I Corinthians 9:16f.: "Woe to me if I do not preach the gospel! For if I do this of my own will, I have a reward; but if not of my own will, I am entrusted with a commission (*oikonomian*)." The Ephesian letter picks this up in 1:10 ("a stewardship [*oikonomian*] for the fulness of time"), a plan by which God will "unite all things in him, things in the heavens and things on earth." This plan and purpose has been entrusted to Paul, "to make all men see what is the plan (*oikonomia*) of the mystery hidden for ages in God who created all things" (3:9). On this basis Paul "became a minister according to the divine office (*oikonomian*) which was given" to him as a messenger to the Gentiles (Col. 1:25).

The second weighty word is *musterion* (mystery): "how the mystery was made known to me by revelation, as I have written briefly" (3:3). The previous writing may be either Colossians 1:26 or Ephesians 1:9f., for both make reference to this mystery. The mystery remains mysterious even after it is revealed. The mystery even deepens; it does not disappear.

Musterion is a very meaningful word, first appearing in the Pauline epistles with reference to the man of sin (II Thess. 2:7), but the most instructive background is found in I Corinthians and Colossians. The mystery of God is mentioned once as the gospel (2:1), but some manuscripts have *marturion* (testimony). The five other references in I Corinthians (2:7; 4:1; 13:2; 14:2; 15:51), however, have reference to secrets disclosed by spiritual media.

(1) *The mystery of God* is the major mystery. The first reference relates the word very closely to the wisdom of God. What the world called *sophia* (wisdom) God made *moria* (folly), and what God revealed as *sophia* the world regarded as *moria*. This makes both an earthly and a heavenly wisdom, one from above and one from below (cf. Jas. 3:15-17). The heavenly wisdom can be grasped only by the spiritually mature, for it is hidden from those dominated by evil spirits (I Cor. 2:6-9), revealed by the Spirit of God much as the spirit of man reveals the thoughts of man (I Cor. 2:10-13), and received by those who have the Spirit (I Cor. 2:14-3:3). The primary difference between the natural man (2:14) and the spiritual man (2:15) is at this point. Even some who have received the Spirit are immature and live like ordinary men who have not received the Spirit; these are the carnal Christians (I Cor. 3:1-3; cf. Rom. 8:12f.).

Paul thought of himself and his fellow workers as "servants of Christ and stewards of the mysteries of God" (1 Cor. 4:1), and this plural usage is found in relation to prophetic powers, knowledge, and a faith that can remove mountains (I Cor. 13:2). The man who speaks in tongues "utters mysteries in the Spirit" (I Cor. 14:2). The manner of the resurrection of the dead was one of the mysteries made known to Paul (I Cor. 15:51), and the salvation of Israel after the fulness of the Gentiles was another mystery (Rom. 11:25), but the primary mystery in the present is God's purpose in the Gentile mission (Rom. 16:25-27).

(2) *The mystery of Christ* is the mystery of the Gentile mission. Paul was made a minster to make known "the mystery hidden for ages and generations but now made manifest to his saints" (Col. 1:26). It was to the saints that God "chose to make known how great among the Gentiles are the riches of the glory of this mystery, which is Christ in you, the hope of glory" (1:27). Paul also strives that the Gentiles may "have all the riches of assured understanding and the knowledge of God's mystery, of Christ, in whom are hid all the treasures of wisdom and knowledge" (2:3). He prayed for an open door "to declare the mystery of Christ" (4:3).

(3) *The mystery of the gospel* includes all that has been said on the mystery of God and Christ. As usual the Ephesian letter uses and polishes the words of the Colossian letter. God has "made known to us in all wisdom and insight the mystery of his will, according to his good purpose which he set forth in Christ, as a plan for the fulness of time, to unite all things in him, things in heaven and things on earth" (1:9f.), and the prayer requested by Paul is "that utterance may be given me in opening my mouth boldly to proclaim the mystery of the gospel" (1:19). The mystery of his will or the mystery of the gospel was God's purpose among the Gentiles.

The stewardship of this mystery came through revelation (*apokalupsis*), and this is the third word of great importance. The mode of this revelation is spiritual. "When you read this you can perceive my insight into the mystery of Christ, which was not made known to the sons of men in other

generations as it has now been revealed to his holy apostles
and prophets by the Spirit" (3:4f.). This is the mode outlined
in I Corinthians 2:6-3:3, but the Christian apostles and
prophets are a special group of charismatic persons to whom
God makes known his mysteries (2:20; 4:11; I Cor. 14:1-5,
24ff.; Acts 11:27f.; 13:1; 14:14). In Colossians 1:26 it was to
"the saints" that the mystery was made known. It has already been pointed out how that these are not Old Testament prophets and the Twelve Apostles. At times the Church
has attempted to quench the Spirit by crushing such persons,
but God seems always to raise up more.

The meaning of this revelation is the secret now disclosed:
"that the Gentiles are fellow heirs (*sugklēronoma*), and fellow members of the body (*sussōma*), and fellow partakers
(*summetocha*) of the promise in Christ Jesus through the
gospel" (3:6, ASV). The little word *nun* (now) in 3:5 is of
great significance, for Paul's thought now turns on this small
pivot: the mystery "has been made known" (*egnoristhē*, 3:
5) that it "might be made known (*gnoristhē*, 3:10). The
Jews had assumed that they were the sole heirs, members,
and partakers, but *now* they must make room for the Gentiles
in the one body of Christ. *Now* a world mission is under way.

The vocabulary of mystery surveyed above continues in the
Pastoral Epistles. A deacon "must hold the mystery of the
faith with a clear conscience" (I Tim. 3:9), and that mystery
of Christ is sung in the hymn which follows immediately
(3:16):

1. He was manifested in the flesh
2. vindicated in the spirit
3.   seen by angels,
4. preached among the nations,
5. believed on in the world
6.   taken up to glory.

This mystery interpreted in chronological order would have
reference to (1) Jesus in the days of his flesh, (2) his
vindication while his spirit was absent from his body between
death and resurrection (cf. I Pet. 3:18), (3) his appearance

to the fallen angels or disobedient spirits in prison (I Pet. 3:19), (4) the preaching to the dead as the nations now in Hades (I Pet. 4:6), (5) belief by those who saw him between resurrection and ascension, and (6) the ascension itself.[3]

Mysteries both good (1:20; 10:7) and evil (17:5) are found in Revelation, and once the idea appears in the Synoptic Gospels (Mk. 4:11; Mt. 13:11; Lk. 8:10).

At one time Protestant theology saw much significance in the influence of the mystery religions on the New Testament, but this has declined in recent years.[4]   In Roman Catholic thought the mystery theology has created a considerable stir, and it is the source of much of the liturgical reform taking place today.[5]

The revelation of the mystery is to be followed by *the proclamation of the mystery* (3:7-13). If there are similarities between this mystery and the Greek religious cults, the so-called mystery religions, there is one distinctive difference. The mystery of the gospel is not to be kept a cultic secret but proclaimed to the world. The Church is no secret order. This mystery is first proclaimed through Paul (3:7-9) and then through the Church (3:10-13).

The ministry of Paul was to proclaim the mystery of the gospel. In a twofold way he was made a minister (*diakonos,* servant): "according (*kata*) to the gift of God's grace" and "according (*kata*) to the working of his power" (3:7). Paul had nothing he had not received (I Cor. 4:7), and he could do nothing apart from "the working of his power" (*tēn energeian tēs dunameōs autou*).

God's grace left the apostle feeling that he was "the very least of all the saints" (3:8). In I Corinthians 15:9 he spoke of himself as "the least of the apostles, unfit to be an apostle,"

---

[3] A summary of views may be found in an essay by R. P. Martin, "Aspects of Worship in the New Testament Church," *Vox Evangelica,* pp. 21-27.

[4] H. A. A. Kennedy, *St. Paul and the Mystery-Religions,* pp. 123-130, represents the positive attitude, but Gunther Wagner, *Das religionsgeschichtliche Problem von Romer 6:1-11,* is more negative.

[5] Odo Casel, *The Mystery of Christian Worship.*

and in II Corinthians 2:11 he declares: "I am not at all inferior to these superlative apostles, even though I am nothing."

The grace that was given was "to preach among the Gentiles the unsearchable riches of Christ, and to make all men see what is the plan of the mystery hidden for ages in God who created all things" (3:9). The word *anexichniaston* (unsearchable), from the negative of *exichniazo*, to track out, means "trackless," for Paul believed that there is no map of the mystery of God that traces all the trails and no explorer who has discovered all the riches of grace. It is all a vast wilderness of wonder with treasures untold.

This is the trackless wilderness in which Paul became lost as he explored the mystery of Israel and found room for the Gentiles. "O the depth of the riches and wisdom and knowledge of God! How unsearchable are his judgments and how inscrutable his ways!" (Rom. 11:33). How can human pride confront this mystery and claim to have reproduced it in all its riches in a petty system of human thought, philosophical or theological?

God's purpose is "to make all men see what is the plan of the mystery hidden for ages in God who created all things" (3:9). That is his purpose: "to make men see!" The infinitive *photisai* (to see) means "to bring to light." Under the domination of the powers of darkness men are blind, so God called the Apostle Paul "to open their eyes, that they may turn from darkness to light and from the power of Satan to God" (Acts 26:18).

The first full-time professor of missions in the English-speaking world, the second in the world, was W. O. Carver of Southern Baptist Theological Seminary, Louisville, Kentucky. For half a century he kept the world mission of the Church before his students, many of whom went to the ends of the earth as heralds of Christ. Few men of the twentieth century were as truly ecumenical in spirit and missionary in vision as this kindly and courageous man.

When at last the end of his earthly pilgrimage had come there was little doubt as to what passage of the New Testament was most appropriate at the memorial service. He had lived his life around Ephesians 3:9 in particular and the Ephesian letter in general, and his *Missions in the Plan of the Ages* had been used of God to help many hear the call to go into the darkness to take the light and thus help fulfil the purpose in the world and in their personal lives. When this vision vanishes there will be darkness again where once there was light. May the light never go out.

At the present the dead hand of human tradition hinders the bright light of biblical truth. Even churchmen fear a fresh study of Holy Scripture lest light break forth to threaten their traditional beliefs and practices. It is time for a new Tyndale to turn men back to the truth of Scripture, for the last prayer of the great translator, as he was strangled to death, is a solemn reminder of the present state: "Lord, open the king of England's eyes." There are eyes today that need to be opened.

The proclamation which began with Paul is to be continued on a cosmic scale in the Church: "that through the church the manifold wisdom of God might now be made known to the principalities and powers in the heavenly places" (3:10). The mission of the Church is more than universal; it is cosmic. The Church has more than a mission; it is a medium, "that through the church the manifold wisdom of God might be made known to the principalities and powers in the heavenly places."

When the Church is viewed as a medium of revelation it must be thought of as the body of Christ created by the Holy Spirit, not as the institution that has so often fallen far short of her mission in the world. Of the three greatest miracles in history (Israel, Christ, and the Church), only Christ has been without spot and blemish; but God was able to accomplish his purpose in the Church. Heresies and schisms delay the completion of the body of Christ and her presentation as a spotless bride, but God does not abandon his purpose.

The manifold (*polupoikilos*) wisdom of God revealed through the Church requires more variety than the crusaders for conformity are willing to recognize. It would be a pity, at least at the present, to pour all Christians into the mold of any one denomination. If, on the other hand, by some great spiritual awakening and renewal, the true insights of all groups plus the new insights which would surely come could be gathered up into one great fellowship of freedom and love, that would be a glimpse of God's ultimate goal even while the church militant bears her witness in a fallen world. That is very near the picture presented by *polupoikilos* (manifold), for it describes "the intricate beauty of an embroidered pattern."[6] An Orphic hymn uses the word to mean "many-sided," and the kindred word *poikilēs* (varied) is used of God's varied (*poikilēs*) grace" (I Pet. 4:10).

The principalities and powers are to be understood against the background of the seven spheres into which the heavenly places or spiritual realm was divided and over which angelic powers ruled. The visible planets were associated with these spheres and ruled by angels. In relation to the cosmic redemption of Christ these powers pass through three stages: they are first created in Christ (Col. 1:16), then they fall into rebellion against Christ and are hostile to his purpose (I Cor. 2:6-8; Rom. 8:38; Eph. 6:12), and finally they are united again and made subject to Christ (Col. 1:20; 2:10, 15; Eph. 1:10, 21; I Pet. 3:22). Such astrological ideas may seem fantastic to contemporary science, but the cosmic significance which the message conveys can be translated into even the most exact current cosmology. The truth of Christ and the truth of science do not contradict.

The role of the Church as the medium through which the wisdom of God is to be made known to the cosmic powers is for the second time proclaimed (cf. 1:21), and the wisdom of God is his "plan for the fulness of time, to unite all things in him [Christ], things in heaven and things on earth" (1:10).

In summary: "This was according to the eternal purpose

6 J. Armitage Robinson, *St. Paul's Epistle to the Ephesians*, p. 80.

which he has realized in Christ Jesus our Lord, in whom we have boldness and confidence of access through our faith in him" (3:11). The plan of all the ages will be realized in a person with whom each believer may have the most personal relation. A more literal translation would be: "we have boldness and access with confidence" (KJV). Boldness (*parrēsia*) means freedom of speech, one of the great benefits of trust in Christ. We are free to speak to the Lord of all history! Access (*prosagogēn*) allows us to come into his very presence (2:18). This we may do with confidence that he will not turn us away but give meaning to our fragmented lives.

With this confidence all difficulties can be surmounted. "So I ask you not to lose heart over what I am suffering for you, which is your glory" (3:13). His sufferings in prison are for their benefit, so they should not be discouraged. "Now rejoice in my sufferings for your sake, and in my flesh I complete what is lacking in Christ's afflictions for the sake of his body, that is, the church" (Col. 1:24). Martyrs are the glory of the Church. As the great Tertullian was to say later: *semen est sanguis Christianorum.*[7] There is no way to discourage Christians with these convictions.

THE POWER OF GOD
(3:14-21)

The purpose of God in Christ is to be accomplished by God's power working in the members of Christ's body, the Church. God's power is appropriated through prayer, both private and corporate, and this is at the very heart of the Ephesian letter. After the great doxology with which the letter opens (1:3-14), there was a great prayer for knowledge; and now the powerful and penetrating parenthesis on the purpose of God is followed by a great prayer for power: the power of God's Spirit (3:14-16) and the power of God's love (3:17-19).

---

[7] "The blood of Christians is seed." *Apology,* 50.

The power of God's Spirit (3:14-16). As Paul gets to the point, the posture of bowing his knees, 3:1 is picked up again: "For this reason I bow my knees before the Father from whom every family in heaven and earth is named" (3:14). Prayer among Pharisees was done standing (Mt. 6:2; Luke 18: 11, 13), and this posture of prayer was also assumed by the disciples of Jesus (Mk. 11:25). Jesus prayed at times prostrate (Mk. 14:35), but the common posture for Paul seemed to be that of kneeling (Acts 9:40; 20:36; 21:5). That is reflected in the phrase "I bow my knees" in this prayer.

Solomon's kneeling at the dedication of the temple (I Kings 8:54), Stephen at his martyrdom (Acts 7:60), Peter at the death of Dorcas (Acts 9:40), Paul's farewells (Acts 20:36; 21:5), and Jesus in Gethsemane (Lk. 22:41) indicate that it was "an expression of deep emotion or earnestness."[8]

In the early Church there were some important writings on prayer. Tertullian, who wrote the first treatise on the subject at the beginning of the third century, indicates that the congregation usually knelt to pray on ordinary days, especially in fasts and stations (23), but on Sundays and between Easter and Pentecost, in light of the resurrection, they stood after the model of the sinner in Luke 18:13.[9] Origen, who wrote the second treatise between 231 and 250, followed the same pattern, but he thought it appropriate for the sick and sailors on a voyage to lie down or sit![10]

Some may think such questions of little importance, since private and mental prayer are emphasized over corporate worship, but there is much value in these suggestions when put into practice. In modern practice it is so easy to stop at meditation, the threshold of prayer, and fail to press on to adoration, confession, thanksgiving, supplication, and intercession when "the Spirit himself intercedes for us with sighs too deep for words" (Rom. 8:26). Even praying in tongues should not be forbidden (1 Cor. 14:5, 18).

8 Francis Foulkes, *The Epistle of Paul to the Ephesians*, p. 101.
9 Earnest Evans, *Tertullian's Tract on the Prayer*, 14.
10 E. G. Jay, *Origen's Treatise on Prayer*, 31. 2f.

The address of the prayer is "to the Father, from whom every family in heaven and on earth is named." The phrase "of our Lord Jesus Christ" is not to be found in the best manuscripts, although it represents the central concept in the New Testament teaching on the fatherhood of God. Addressing God as Father in Christian prayer (2:18; 3:14) is most fully expressed in the prayer often called "the Our Father" (Mt. 6:8-15). Three times each day the early Christian prayed this prayer (*Didache,* 8:3). This was perhaps at the third, sixth, and ninth hours of the day (Tertullian, *On Prayer,* 25).

God as Father of all is beautifully expressed in the play on words in the Greek text: "I bow my knees to the *patera* (Father), from whom every *patria* (family) in heaven and on earth is named." The belief in God as *Patēr Pantōn* (father of all), that looms so large in this letter, includes both his creative and redeeming activity, both the families "in heaven and on earth." This is discussed later at 4:6, but here it is the focus of prayer.

Patria (family, fatherhood) is any group (tribe or nation) descended from the same father. God as Father is the prototype of all patriarchs, being the creator of all tribes and nations and offering redemption to all in Christ (1:5). At the throne of grace all men learn that they are brothers and that God is the patriarch of all faithful peoples, Father of all. Therefore "call no man your father on earth, for you have one Father, who is in heaven" (Mt. 23:9).

Prayer is power in a twofold way: as the power of the Spirit (3:14-16) and as the power of love (3:17-19). The prayer to the *Pater* prepares the way for the first petition: "that according to the riches of his glory he may grant you to be strengthened with might through his Spirit in the inner man" (3:16).

The spiritual resources of power are measured by "the riches of his glory." In the first prayer of the Ephesian letter God is called "the Father of glory" (1:17), and that has been interpreted as a reference to the Shekinah glory that came to dwell in the flesh of Christ. In that light "the riches of his glory" would have reference to "the riches of the glory of this mystery, which is Christ in you, the hope of glory" (Col. 1:27). God's mystery, hidden and at the same time revealed through the Spirit, is "Christ, in whom are hid all the treasures of wisdom and knowledge" (2:3).

God's spiritual reservoir, stored up for the seasons of refreshing, finds expression in Longfellow's *Tales of a Wayside Inn*:

> *As torrents in summer,*
> *Half dried in their channels,*
> *Suddenly rise, though the*
> *Sky is still cloudless,*
> *For rain has been falling*
> *Far off at their fountains;*
>
> *So hearts that are fainting*
> *Grow full to o'erflowing,*
> *And they that beheld it*
> *Marvel, and know not*
> *That God at their fountains*
> *Far off has been raining!*[11]

This spiritual region, their fountain, in which the power of God is appropriated through the Spirit, is the inner man. The later contrast (4:23f.) between the old man (*palaion anthropos*) and the new man (*kainon anthropos*), man out of Christ and man in Christ, is not the same as that between the outer man (*exō anthropos*) and inner man (*esō anthropos*). The outer man is physical man, the visible and transient creature of time that does not pass away. "Wherefore we faint not; but though our outward man is decaying, yet our inward man is renewed day by day" (II Cor. 4:16, ASV).

The inner man is a reality even under the law and the "fallen state." "For I delight in the law of God after the inward man: but I see a different law in my members, warring against the law of my mind, and bringing me into captivity under the law of sin which is in my members. Wretched man that I am! Who shall deliver me out of the body of this death?" The

[11] *The Complete Poetical Works of Henry Wadsworth Longfellow*, p. 301.

body of death is the same as "the body of sin," "the old man"
that is "done away" when one becomes a member of the body
of Christ (Rom. 6:6), yet the inner man is the real man even
while he is in "the body of death" and has not yet put on the
new man. The inner man is renewed when the new man is
put on.

The inner man is renewed and delivered from the slavery
of sin by the Spirit, and the new life is lived as one is "strengthened with might through his Spirit in the inner man" (Eph.
3:16). This process of the renewal of life through the Spirit
is the theme of one of the profoundest chapters in all the Bible
(Rom. 8). The law of the Spirit delivers from the law of sin
and death which the law of Moses can bring to consciousness
but from which it is unable to deliver (8:1-4). The mind of
the Spirit, mind renewed by the Spirit, pleases God, a thing
impossible for the mind of the flesh, the mind of self-centered
man (8:5-7). The indwelling Spirit, being the Spirit that
raised the body of Jesus, will raise our bodies after death
(8:8-11).

The life of the Spirit, in contrast to the life of the flesh, is
given by the Spirit of life (8:12-13), and the leading of the
Spirit is the chief characteristic of the children of God (8:14-
17). All this is the first-fruits of the Spirit (8:18-25) to be
followed by the full harvest of cosmic redemption, and prayer
by which this transforming power continues to work in the
Christian is the intercession of the Spirit (8:26f.).

The renewal of the Church always begins with the renewal
of man. If one looks for the secret in the extraordinary life of
D. L. Moody he is most likely to find it in his Spirit-filled experience with God. In 1871 this happened:

> A strangely changed Moody walked down a New York street
> one night in November. He had never been drunk with wine
> in his life. But now, he knew the exultation which Satan's
> counterfeit imitated. Every time he stepped, one foot said
> "glory" and the other responded "hallelujah." Suddenly he

12 Richard Ellsworth Day, *Bush Aglow*, p. 136.

sobbed, "Oh God, why don't you *compel* me to walk close to thee, always? Deliver me from myself! Take absolute sway! Give me Thy Holy Spirit!"[12]

It was this experience that transformed his preaching from sawdust to an artesian stream. And the God of D. L. Moody still lives.

The power of God's love (3:17-19). The corollary to the Spirit of God is the love of God. "God's love has been poured into our hearts through the Holy Spirit which has been given to us" (Rom. 5:5). He who does not have the love of God does not have the Spirit of God, for the two are always found together. The opening of the self required to receive the Spirit of God opens also to receive the love of God, the self-giving, down-pouring, unmerited gift of God.

It is interesting that Charles G. Finney describes an experience with God very similar to that described by D. L. Moody, yet he speaks of it more in terms of love than of the Spirit. In a face to face encounter with Jesus Christ Finney was filled with love by the Holy Spirit. He says:

> But as I turned and was about to take a seat by the fire, I received a mighty baptism of the Holy Ghost. Without any expectation of it, without ever having the thought in my mind that there was any such thing for me, without any recollection that I had even heard the thing mentioned by any person in the world, the Holy Spirit descended upon me in a manner that seemed to go through me, body and soul. I could feel the impression, like a wave of electricity going through and through me. Indeed it seemed to come in waves and waves of liquid love; for I could not express it in any other way. It seemed like the very breath of God.[13]

It is as fatal as it is false to dismiss such testimony as some sort of mental illness divorced from ultimate reality. It is the really real itself that has happened, and the renewal of the Church rests on this reality.

The power of God's love is the second petition in this prayer for power: "that Christ may dwell in your hearts through faith; that you, being rooted and grounded in love,

---

[13] *Memoirs of Rev. Charles G. Finney*, p. 20.

may have power to comprehend with all the saints what is the breadth and length and height and depth, and to know the love of Christ which surpasses knowledge, that you may be filled with all the fulness of God" (3:17-19). Three infinitives indicate steps by which the love of Christ is appropriated: *katoikēsai* (to dwell), *katalabesthai* (to comprehend), *gnōnai* (to know).

The prayer for Christ "to dwell" in their hearts employs the same verb that speaks of the *plērōma* (fulness) dwelling in both the fleshly (Col. 1:19) and the mystical (2:9) body of Christ, and the noun has already been used in the Ephesian letter for the dwelling of God in his holy temple the church (2:22). It has reference to the permanent abode of Christ in the heart, in contrast to *paroikein* (to sojourn for a while). May the Christ who came to dwell permanently in the body of Christ, beginning in the fleshly body and continuing in the mystical body, make his permanent abode in our hearts. This is the general meaning of the prayer.

The eyes of the heart (*kardia*) may be enlightened (1:18), so that it makes melody to the Lord (5:19, cf. Col. 3:16) and may be single in devoted service (6:5, cf. Col. 3:22). It is the seat of all emotion, thought, and will and may be encouraged by Christian friends (6:23; Col. 2:2; 4:8). It may also become hardened and calloused by darkness and disobedience to God (4:17-19). It is the permanent abode of Christ that dispels the darkness and softens the heart before the Lord.

The permanence of Christ's abode and continuance in faith are inseparable corollaries. If there is no permanent faith there is no permanent abode, for a saving faith is a steadfast faith. "And you, who once were estranged and hostile in mind, doing evil deeds, he has now reconciled in his body of flesh by his death, in order to present you holy and blameless and irreproachable before him, provided that you continue in the faith, stable and steadfast, nor shifting from the hope of the gospel which you heard, which has been preached to every creature under heaven, and of which I, Paul, become a minister" (Col. 1:21-23). Colossae was devastated by an earthquake in A.D. 60-61, so Paul calls for a faith that can withstand the tremors of temptation (cf. Lk. 8:13; I Cor. 10:6-13; Heb. 3:12). "As therefore you received Christ Jesus the Lord, so live in him, rooted and built up in him and established in the faith, just as you were taught, abounding in thanksgiving" (Col. 2:6f.).

Permanent faith is a life of faith in which "we walk by faith, not by sight" (II Cor. 5:6). "I have been crucified with Christ; and it is no longer I who live, but Christ who lives in me; and the life I now live in the flesh I live by faith in the Son of God, who loved me and gave himself for me" (Gal. 2:20).

The prayer "to comprehend" relates the believer to both Christ and other Christians. Comprehension of love is possible only when one is "rooted and grounded in love" (3:17). Paul longed for the Colossians to be "knit together in love" (2:2) and to "be rooted and built up in him and established in the faith" (2:7), but here one is to be rooted in love as a tree in the soil and grounded as a pillar in a temple. Stability in both faith and love are marks of a true believer.

Steadfast love does not exclude others who love the Lord Jesus in sincerity. Indeed it must include others if it is "the love of Christ." We comprehend love only in the community of love "with all the saints." Love is an abstraction until we are related to one another in a life of sharing and concern, a "common life in the body of Christ" (the title of a great book by L. S. Thornton).

No one can measure the love of Christ alone (cf. 1:15). It is intended for all even as the *plērōma* (fulness) of Christ fills "his body, the fulness of him who fills all in all" (1:23), for it is the purpose of Christ "to fill all things" (4:10). Comprehension of "the breadth and length and height and depth" of Christ's love includes no less than all, and the fulness fills all. The astrological ideas of "height" and "depth" are found in Romans 8:39, but this is the only place in the New Testament where all four dimensions of the universe are mentioned.

It is not a lesson in astrology, but it is good theology, the theology of the boundless love of Christ.

Irenaeus of Lyon saw the four dimensions of the love of God in the cosmic cross of Christ. "For as we lost it by means of a tree, by means of a tree again it was made manifest to all, showing the height, the length, the breadth, the depth in itself" (*Against Heresies,* V.17.4).

F. W. Faber shames our narrowness and rigorism with the words that are sung all too complacently:

> *For the love of God is broader*
> *Than the measure of man's mind;*
> *And the heart of the Eternal*
> *Is most wonderfully kind.*

> *But we make His love too narrow*
> *By false limits of our own;*
> *And we magnify His strictness*
> *With a zeal He will not own.*

The prayer "to know" joins "the love of Christ" and "the fulness of God" (3:19). Knowledge (*gnosis*) was a highly prized spiritual gift among some Christians. In Corinth it was so highly prized that the higher gift of love was neglected, so Paul goes into some details about the three stages (I Cor. 8) of spiritual growth (conscience, knowledge, and love), and for him the greatest of these was love (I Cor. 13). Knowledge without love can cause a weak brother to perish (I Cor. 8:11), so it is very important for knowledge to be elevated to the higher level of love.

The elevation takes place when we come "to know the love of Christ which surpasses knowledge." Love is both greater and better than knowledge, for knowledge without love makes for pride. "Love is patient and kind, love is not jealous or boastful; it is not arrogant or rude" (I Cor. 13:4). This supremacy of love was never lost even in the most extreme Christian Gnostic, Clement of Alexandria, for his four stages of spiritual life were faith, knowledge, love, and the heavenly inheritance (*Stromateis,* VII. X).

Knowledge of " the love of Christ" makes it possible for one to "be filled with all the fulness of God." Does this mean that the supernatural powers that come to dwell in the fleshly body of Christ come also to dwell in the mystical body, the Church? Apparently this is the view expressed elsewhere: "For in him the whole fulness of deity dwells bodily, and you have come to fulness of life in him" (Col. 2:9f.). The powers made manifest in Jesus, when people knew his words were God's words and his works were God's works, now descend upon the mystical body and give power to her witness in the world.

Being "filled with all the fulness of God" is not some sudden thing that takes place in the individual and is all over. It "grows with a growth that is from God" (Col. 2:19). It is attained when Christ has filled all things (Eph. 4:10) and the body of Christ, now in process of growth, has arrived at "mature manhood, to the measure of the stature of the fulness of Christ" (4:13).

A doxology (3:20f.). The short doxology with which this chapter concludes brings the prayer for power into union with the purpose of God. "Now to him who by the power at work within us is able to do far more abundantly than all we ask or think, to him be glory in the church and in Christ Jesus to all generations, for ever and ever. Amen" (cf. Rom. 16:25-27; Jude 24f.). God's power is equal to his purpose.

God's power in inward and incomprehensible. It does not come as some irresistible force from the outside, overwhelming the will and dispensing with the mind, but as a dynamic and persuasive movement of the Spirit and love of God that molds the meaningless life of man into the meaningful purpose of God, the purpose that unites all things in heaven and on earth.

Its incomprehensible nature may be seen in the literal translation of the statement about the ability of God: that he "is able to do exceeding abundantly above all we ask or think" (ASV), language that A. T. Robertson thinks is piling "Pelion on Ossa."[14] God's ability does not remove man's

[14] *Word Pictures in the New Testament,* IV (1931), 534.

responsibility, but it should remove man's despair at arriving at the goal of God.

God's glory seems always to have some connection with the Shekinah glory that came to dwell in Christ and continues to dwell in the Church. It may be that "in the church" and "in Christ Jesus" mean the same, but it seems that Christ Jesus includes more than the Church. As the circle goes beyond the Church there is that which is "in Christ Jesus" which is not "in the church." The larger circle would be the whole creation (*ta panta*).

God's glory, his personal presence with his people, never ends. In the great doxology with which the Ephesian letter begins the whole process of salvation history is ascribed to the "praise of his glory," but this briefer doxology includes both history and eternity. A generation (*genea*) is a subdivision of an age (*aiōn*), but "all generations, for ever and ever" (*pasas tas geneas tou aiōnos tōn aiōnōn*) embraces all time and eternity. This is the arena of God's glory, his personal presence, in which his purpose will be achieved by his power.

In our generation his glorious presence will be made manifest according to the power and love that the Church allows to work in her life and members. The glory that was in Christ from all eternity is made manifest in the Church and in the world as the love that unites Christ to God comes to unite Christians to God and to one another (cf. John 17).

What an overwhelming vision of the purpose of God! God creates all that is not deity (*ta panta*), but much of it falls into discord and becomes alienated from him. How is he to unite all and to reconcile all to himself again? His first step is to fill one man, who is also his eternal Son, with all his supernatural powers (*plērōma*), then the supernatural powers that dwelt in this fleshly body, by the exaltation of the crucified Son, come to dwell in many fleshly bodies and to unite them in one mystical body, the Church, and after that to unite all things visible and invisible, in heaven and on earth, under the headship of him who is the head of the Church, Jesus

Christ our Lord. This is the purpose of God, a plan for the Church ever to have before her as she confronts the practical problems of a fallen order and the hostility of estranged men, dominated by principalities and powers.

Chapter Four:

THE CHRISTIAN CALLING
(4:1-5:20)

The late W. O Carver thought the theme of Christian calling to be dominant in the Ephesian letter, so he gave his exposition the title: *The Glory of God in the Christian Calling.*
In this section at least his insight was sound, for the call to
glorify God in the Christian life is clear and comprehensive.

Calling may be a universal invitation extended to all men,
even when many reject the call ("for many are called, but few
are chosen," Mt. 22:14). On the other hand, it may be confined to those who accept the salvation and are thereby the
same as the chosen ("and those whom he predestined he also
called," Rom. 8:30, cf. Hos. 11:1; Isa. 43:1). A third concept
of calling has reference to service. Some are called to service
who are not called to salvation, as in the case of Cyrus (Isa.
45:4), but more often those called to service are the same as
those called to salvation. In much evangelical theology this
call to service is confined to a special group of those who are
saved, as one may speak of a "call" to be a minister or a missionary. The present trend to underemphasize this thought is
cause for concern, for it means the muffling of the prophetic
consciousness (Amos 7:14; Jer. 1:4f.; I Cor. 1:1), a situation
that will reduce all preachers to priests of the *status quo.*

The call that comes to the whole "company of the committed," to use Elton Trueblood's phrase, does not require a
rejection of the prophetic call to certain "gifted" Christians.

A survey will show that most, if not all prophetic personalities have experienced this prophetic "call," and a sad situation will settle about us if this continues to be de-emphasized. A call to the laity, the whole people of God, is good, but this is not all. It is, however, the chief consideration in this section on the Christian calling. It is a call that comes to all Christians by the sole fact that they are Christians. Disobedience to this calling is Christian disobedience on the part of every person who pushes the call aside.

THE CALL TO WALK WORTHILY
(4:1-16)

"I therefore, the prisoner in the Lord, beseech you to walk worthily of the calling, wherwith ye were called" (4:1, ASV). Even in prison Paul is "in the Lord," and he is acutely conscious of the threat of schism in the body of Christ, the Church (cf. I Cor. 12:25). It is unworthy of the Christian calling to promote and perpetuate "schism in the body," local or universal. A worthy walk is a walk in unity, and this has two stages.

The unity of the Spirit (4:3). This is the chief concept of 4:1-6. The unity of the Spirit means far more than an inward unity in the sphere of the human spirit. It is a unity created by the Holy Spirit, both inward and outward, both spiritual and organic in the fulness of its manifestation. No false antithesis of spirit and body, the relic of Cartesian dualism, exists in the New Testament.

The unity of the Spirit *is* our Christian calling, for to walk worthily of our calling is to walk "with all lowliness and meekness, with patience, forbearing one another in love, eager to maintain the unity of the Spirit in the bonds of peace" (4:1-3). Lowliness and meekness (*tapeinophrosunē* and *prautēs*) are the very opposite of haughtiness and self-assertion. It was Jesus who was "meek and lowly in heart" (Matt. 11:29, ASV), and these twin virtues displace pride, the primary barrier to Christian unity. One of the historic sermons preached annually at Oxford University in the Church of St. Mary the Virgin is on pride. It was originally intended for young ministers, but it would be profitable for all churches and Christians to hear a frequent sermon on this subject.

Patience and forbearance follow after lowliness and meekness. Long-suffering (KJV) is perhaps a better translation of *makrothumia* than patience (RSV), for it holds out until the broken relation is remedied. The Lord is "longsuffering to you-ward, not wishing that any perish, but that all should come to repentance" (II Pet. 3:9). It is this quality that promotes unity among Christians. Forbearance (*anechomenoi*) has also the quality of endurance to the end, and that is why it is done "in love." "Love suffereth long. . . . Love never faileth" (I Cor. 13:4, 8, ASV), and in the end the harmony experienced by loving hearts will unite all in Christ (1:10).

When love has been fully experienced in our relationship with God and with man an eagerness (*spoudē*) settles about even the smallest acts of love. It is a blazing zeal that thaws the ice of isolation and warms cold hearts until they are one. Once unity is won, it must be maintained, guarded, and watched lest the cold winds of unconcern blow out the flame. As long as the fire burns, "the bond of peace," the ligament of love, holds all together. In Colossians 3:12ff. the seven garments of grace are insufficient until love, "which binds everything together in perfect harmony," is "put on."

The unity of the Spirit is also our confession. "There is one body and one Spirit, just as you were called to the one hope that belongs to your call, one Lord, one faith, one baptism, one God and Father of all, who is above all and through all and in all" (4:4-6). Belief in one God in the Old Testament brought together the one people of God, and this is summarized in the Shema: "Hear, O Israel: The LORD our God is one LORD" (Deut. 6:4). In the Greek period, when disunity threatened, unity became a prophetic hope: "The LORD will become king over all the earth; on that day the LORD will be one and his name one" (Zech. 14:9).

Sources for the sevenfold oneness in Ephesians 4:4-6 appear in other places. Out of polytheism people come to worship "one God, the Father, from whom are all things and for whom we exist, and one Lord, Jesus Christ, through whom are all things and through whom we exist" (I Cor. 8:6). Christian communion is the sign of this oneness: "Because there is one loaf, we who are many are one body, for we all partake of the same loaf" (I Cor. 10:17). It was baptism that brought us into this oneness with Christ and one another: "For just as the body is one and has many members, and all the members of the body, though many, are one body, so it is with Christ. For by one Spirit we were all baptized into one body—Jews or Greeks, slaves or free—and all were made to drink of one Spirit" (I Cor. 12:12f.).

The first trilogy in the sevenfold oneness speaks of "one body and one Spirit, just as you were called to one hope that belongs to your call" (4:4). It is possible that a briefer confession of visible and invisible unity appears in the words "one body and one Spirit" (*hen sōma kai hen pneuma*), and to this the other articles of oneness have been added to make the sevenfold splendor. Any effort to argue for more than "one body," as if each congregation of Christians is a separate body, is artificial and absurd. To primitive Christianity this would have sounded more like polytheism than the worship of one Lord, and the suggestion that Christ has thousands of bodies would have struck New Testament disciples as a strange gospel.

Only once is *sōma* used in reference to the Church without the article, and there it means Christ's body (*sōma Christou*, I Cor. 12:27), not "a body," but some have sought support for their isolationism in "an ecclesiology of the missing *to*." More is missing in this mentality than the article *to*; the whole point of the New Testament Church has been missed.[1] All the house churches and all the city churches

---

[1] The Roman Catholic theologian Emile Mersch makes this same error in his famous book on *The Whole Christ*, pp. 116f.

make one world church, the one body of Christ, and each part is to build up the whole.

There is only one visible body as there is only one Spirit. A plurality of bodies is as impossible as a plurality of spirits. Many spirits would be spiritism, many so-called "gods" and many so-called "lords" (I Cor. 8:5), but there can be only "one Spirit" as there is "one God, the Father" and "one Lord, Jesus Christ" (I Cor. 8:6). If one insists on "a local body" alone, so that there would be thousands of bodies, he should be consistent and contend for "a local Spirit" and thousands of spirits. The body is localized in thousands of places as the Spirit is localized in thousands of people, but there is in all places and in all faithful people "one body, one Spirit."

The "one hope that belongs to your call" belongs to those "who first hoped in Christ" and "know what is the hope to which he has called" us (1:12, 18). Our hope is "our inheritance," and God has given the Holy Spirit as a guarantee and foretaste "until we acquire possession of it" (1:14). Without Christ we had "no hope" and were "without God in the world" (2:12). "My hope is built on nothing less than Jesus blood and righteousness" (Edward Motyl).

The second triology in this sevenfold unity is "one Lord, one faith, one baptism" (4:5). The "one Lord" rules out the worship of the many so-called "gods" and so-called "lords" (I Cor. 8:5). To worship other supernatural powers after one has come to believe that "all the fulnes of God was pleased to dwell" in Christ is to be disqualified (Col. 1:19; 2:18). If "all the treasures of wisdom and knowledge" (Col. 2:23) are hidden in Christ, what need is there to seek others?

The "one faith" is the confession "that Jesus Christ is Lord" (Phil. 2:11). None can do this but by the Holy Spirit (I Cor. 12:3), but the Spirit that enables one to believe this binds all together in one belief. Had this one faith never been born there would be no one body and the New Testament would have never been written.

In the "one baptism" this "one faith" is confessed (Rom. 10:9f.). Disputes about one mode were unknown in the New

Testament faith. Immersion indeed was the primary mode for all Christians until the fourteenth century, although the secondary mode of affusion was used in cases of necessity, but the oneness of baptism is found in its meaning. "For as many of you as were baptized into Christ have put on Christ. There is neither Jew nor Greek, there is neither male nor female; for you are all one in Christ Jesus" (Gal. 3:27f.). If this "one baptism" with all the fulness of its meaning could be recovered in our time, our stammering tongues would be loosed in testimony and our stubborn wills would bend in obedience to "confess that Jesus Christ is Lord, to the glory of God the Father" (Phil. 2:11).

Belief in the one God, expressed also in a trilogy ("above all and through all and in all"), brings Christian unity to the peak of perfection. Against the background of the Old Testament monotheism already mentioned it would be unthinkable for New Testament faith to make room for more than "one God." In the light of the person, work, and teachings of our Lord Jesus Christ this "one God" can be no other than "the Father."

As "Father of all" he draws all his children together around himself. The "us" of 4:6 in the RSV and the "you" of the KJV are not in the original Greek, but this is perhaps the focus of God's fatherhood in this context. God is Father of all who are members of Christ's one mystical body, whether they be Jew or Greek. In his eternal relation he is "the God and Father of our Lord Jesus Christ" (II Cor. 1:3), and by adoption he had made those his sons who receive his Spirit in their hearts (Gal. 4:6). In creation, not in the redemptive sense, he is "the Father, from whom are all things and for whom we exist" (I Cor. 8:6). It is important to make these three distinctions in God's fatherhood: by nature, by adoption, by creation.

Much confusion also exists over the failure to balance God's transcendence and God's immanence. Biblical thought never identifies God with All. That would be pantheism (the idea that God is all), but there is the clear teaching that all things exist in God (a view at times called panentheism). Epimenides, the Greek poet and philosopher from Crete, said: "In him we live and move and have our being." This is accepted without qualification in Acts 17:28. God is transcendent indeed ("above all"), but he is also omnipresent ("through all") and immanent ("in all"). At the present time a furious controversy rages over a book by John A. T. Robinson (*Honest to God*, S.C.M. Press, 1963), and much of the controversy grows out of a lack of balance. Ephesians 4:6 supplies that balance but it is present also in Isaiah 57:15; Psalms 139:7f.; Acts 17:22-31; John 4:23f.; and in other biblical passages.

God as *Patēr Pantōn* (Father of all) is further protected against pantheism by the pronounced trinitarian pattern that pervades the Ephesian letter. The trinitarian pattern is no argument against Pauline authorship, for two clear examples are found in the Corinthian letters. As gifts of the Spirit are introduced Paul speaks of "the same Spirit," "the same Lord," and "the same God" (I Cor. 12:4-6). A trinitarian benediction is at the end of II Corinthians: "The grace of the Lord Jesus Christ and the love of God and the fellowship of the Holy Spirit be with you all" (13:13).

A summary of the trinitarian pattern in the Ephesian letter may be seen in the following passages:

1. The praise of God (1:6, 12, 14): the great doxology.
2. The temple of God (2:18): "in one Spirit," "through him" (Christ), "to the Father."
3. The fulness of God (3:14-19): "Spirit" (3:16), "Christ" (3:17), "God" (3:19).
4. The unity of God (4:4-6): "one Spirit," "one Lord," "one God."
5. The worship of God (5:19): psalms addressed to God, hymns about Christ, and spiritual songs sung in the Spirit.

The formulation of the Holy Trinity as one name is first found in "the great commission" (Mt. 28:19), and here Eusebius furnishes a textual variation (Nestle's Greek text), but the foundation for such a formulation is surely to be found in the two passages in the Corinthian letters and the five in the Ephesian letter.

The unity of the faith (4:7-16). The unity of the Spirit (4:3), the unity created by the Spirit, leads logically to the unity of faith (4:13), for oneness of fellowship bears fruit in oneness of belief. This unity of the faith is first received as a spiritual gift (4:7-10). Spiritual gifts (*charismata*) as functions in the body of Christ (nine examples of which are attributed to the Spirit in I Cor. 12:8-11) flow easily to become persons, eight of which follow in I Corinthians 12:28-30. The seven gifts of Romans 12:6-8 are still looked upon as functions, but God has assigned these functions to persons (12:3). In the gift (*dōrea*) of Christ in Ephesians 4:7-11 the functions have been measured out to members of the body so that functions and persons are the same.

As Moses, according to the rabbinical exegesis of Psalm 68:18, went up to Mount Sinai to receive the law as gifts *for* men, so Christ ascends to give gifts *to* men. With Christ "he ascended" only after he had first "descended" into the lower parts of the earth" (*ta katōtera tēs gēs*). Some interpret the descent to be into the earth down below the heavens, but others see here a doctrine of Christ's descent into Hades (cf. I Pet. 3:19; 4:6). The reference to those "under the earth" (*katachthoniōn*, 2:20) in the servant hymn of Philippians 2:5-11 plus the concept of captives in Colossians 2:15 makes possible a descent doctrine in Ephesians 4:9, but this is not central in the thought of the context. The central thought is Christ as the giver of gifts "that he might fill all things" (*ta panta*), the whole created order of things.

After the unity of the faith has been received as a spiritual gift, it must be achieved through spiritual growth (4:11-16). It is both a gift and task, *Gabe* and *Aufgabe* as the Germans say. The gift is fourfold. He first gives "some apostles" — not the Twelve, but apostles like "the apostles Barnabas and Paul" (Acts 14:14) who are sent forth to plant the gospel for the first time in a place. Already these "apostles and prophets" have been mentioned in the Ephesian letter (2:20; 3:5), and they are found also in the Acts (13:1; 14:14). The prophet was of special importance in Corinth (I Cor. 14). The third group, "evangelists," are missionaries to the unconverted after the church has been established; "home missionaries"! The prophets were to build the Church planted by the apostles. The "pastors and teachers" (*tous de poimenas kai didaskalous*) formed one group, not two, and these two functions later became the twofold function of the presbyter-bishop (Acts 20:17, 28; I Tim. 3:1f.; 5:17). Pastor (*poimēn*) is the function of overseeing the flock, teacher that of instructing the flock. Those called pastors today would have been called presbyters (elders) in most of the early churches. It was not until the second century, in the letters of Ignatius, that the bishop became the title for the chief presbyter in the presbytery (but see I Tim. 4:14).

The spiritual growth achieved through this spiritual gift includes all members of the body. It is not the intention of Christ that those included in the fourfold gift do all the work of the Christian ministry. They are to equip the saints so that they can join in the work of the ministry. The RSV translation would suggest three things done of the fourfold gift ("for the equipment of the saints, for the work of the ministry, for the building of the body of Christ"), but the Greek would suggest only two: to (*pros*) equip the saints for (*eis*) the work of ministry, for (*eis*) building up the body of Christ." The immediate intention is to equip the saints, but the ultimate intention is to build the body, the Church, not the kingdom as many often say.

This spiritual growth is twofold. One form is growth in knowledge (4:13f.), and this comes in two stages. The final stage is manhood, "when we all attain to the unity of the faith and of the knowledge of the Son of God, to mature manhood, to the measure of the stature of the fulness of Christ" (4:13). This is a collective manhood, more than the maturity of each separate member of Christ's body. What has been received as a gift is achieved as a goal, when the new humanity has been completed in the completeness of Christ. The Church will reach mature manhood when we all (*hoi pantes*) are "filled with all the fulness of God" (3:19), when the fulness that dwelt in the fleshly body of Christ dwells fully in his mystical body, the Church. This is "the stature of the fulness of Christ."

The first stage of knowledge is childhood. In this stage we continue until we are no longer "children, tossed to and fro and carried about with every wind of doctrine, by the cunning of men, by their craftiness in deceitful wiles" (4:14). The period of growth from childhood to manhood is a time of great danger for the Church. Immature individualism needs to be overcome in collective maturity. Metaphors from sailing and gambling point up the perils of immaturity. The ship of childhood is tossed back and forth and round and round in the winds of new ideas. Gospel gamblers throw the dice of doctrine about in cunning and crafty ways that deceive the immature individual. Their error is the very opposite of the truth.

Growth in knowledge needs to be accompanied by growth in love (4:15f.). It is not enough to speak the truth that men may grow in knowledge; truth needs to be spoken in love. Lack of love may create stubborn resistance even to that which men know to be truth. It takes more than truth to transform the heart. By "speaking the truth in love, we are to grow up in every way into him who is the head, into Christ, from whom the whole body is joined and knit together by every joint with which it is supplied, when each part is working properly, makes bodily growth and upbuilds itself in love" (4:15f.). Forbearance, speaking, and building all require the warmth of love (4:2, 15f.).

The physiological metaphor gathers up the ideas of Christ as the head (Col. 1:18; 2:19) and Christians as members of his body (I Cor. 12:12-26) and portrays a body as "joined" in a harmony similar to the earlier metaphor of the temple (2:21). As both building and body the Church belongs to Christ, and its growth depends on what he supplies (cf. Col.

2:19). The cohesion and completeness of the body come from Christ.

THE CALL TO WALK DIFFERENTLY
(4:17-24)

"This I say therefore, and testify in the Lord, that ye no longer walk as the Gentiles also walk" (4:17, ASV). He who is "the prisoner in the Lord" (4:1, ASV) is also ready to testify in the Lord" (4:17). In mystical union with Christ one can do no other than protest against Gentile paganism as a standard proper for Christian conduct. The protest portrays pagan conduct in terms of the old man (4:17-19) and Christian conduct in terms of the new man (4:22-24). An interlude on the relation between "Christ" and "Jesus" serves as a transition from one type of life to the other.

The old man (4:17-19). The portrait of the old man has three features: a vain mind, a hard heart, and an evil conduct. His vanity or futility of mind is due to the absence of God from his thoughts. Apart from knowledge of the true God who has revealed himself in Jesus Christ, life is futile and frustrating, without meaning and purpose.

This human condition arose when those who "knew God . . . did not honor him as God or give thanks to him, for they became vain in their thinking and their senseless minds were darkened" (Rom. 1:21). Ungodliness was followed by unrighteousness, "since they did not see fit to acknowledge God, God gave them up to a base mind and to improper conduct" (Rom. 1:28). This base or reprobate mind remains until it is renewed by a transforming experience in which men "prove what is the will of God, what is good and acceptable and perfect" (Rom. 12:2). The reprobate and renewed minds differ as the old man differs from the new man.

The old man is "darkened" in his "understanding" (*dianoia*), the process by which he reasons with his mind (*nous*). Unbelief and rebellion bring darkness that can be dispelled only when men believe and have "the eyes of their hearts enlightened" (Eph. 1:18). It is a great mistake to confine sin to the misuse of man's body; the mind also is misused and distorted by turning from the light to darkness.

This vanity of mind has the conditions of alienation and ignorance. Pagan life "alienated from the life of God" is no authentic life. It is inauthentic, a contradiction in the true nature of man, a deviation from his intended destiny. Alienation from God is alienation from abundant life. The ignorance (*agnoia*) in this state of alienation is pardonable, for God overlooks the *agnoia* (Acts 17:30) that is due to human circumstances, invincible ignorance, the *obex* of Roman Catholic theology.

However, the hard heart is a type of culpable ignorance (*agnosia*), "the ignorance (*agnosia*) of foolish men" (I Pet. 2:15). This is the hardness of heart that plunged man into darkness, alienation and *agnoia* (pardonable ignorance). Man's hardness of heart leaves him calloused, "past feeling" (ASV). This calloused condition was not caused by conditions beyond his control, for even pagans are left without excuse when the light that shines in the order of creation (Rom. 1:18-23) and in every human conscience (Rom. 2:14-16) is rejected. According to the knowledge they have, they are responsible to God for their sins. Much, however, is due to their darkness, alienation, and pardonable ignorance, and this God overlooks (Acts 17:30).

Out of this vanity of mind and hardness of heart comes evil conduct. "For from within, out of the heart of man, come evil thoughts, fornication, theft, murder, adultery, coveting, wickedness, deceit, licentiousness, envy, slander, pride, foolishness" (Mk. 7:21f.). The features of the old man appear in pagans when "they have become callous and have given themselves up to licentiousness, greedy to practice every kind of uncleanness" (4:19).

Licentiousness (*aselgeia*) is indecent and outrageous conduct that is shocking even to the general public. It is uncontrolled lewdness, a type of animal behavior. Such conduct embraces "every kind of uncleanness" (4:19). The word *pleonexia* (greediness) summarizes the pagan life of the old man, for it has reference to greed of any type (Col. 3:5), especially the type displayed in ruthless disregard for the person and property of others. The dominant motive of *plenoexia* is to satisfy itself, with little thought of consequences, whether this be in sex or in some other form of sensual satisfaction.

Pagan religion practiced a form of sacramental fornication. The temple of worship and the house of prostitution were often the same. According to the standards of Christian conduct this seems incredible, but much paganism continues to penetrate into practice. Even Elmer Gantry is not altogether an invention of the imagination, and it is time for Tertullian and Savonarola to thunder again. Tertullian was in error when he identified adultery with apostasy, but his moral indignation needs to be recovered (*On Modesty*, 1).

"You did so learn Christ!—assuming that you have heard about him and were taught in him, as the truth is in Jesus" (4:20f.). Christ and conduct are related to Jesus. Any conduct that claims a heavenly "Christ" that has no relation to the historical life and sacrificial death of Jesus is based on a false teaching. Truth is that which is no longer hidden, and Christian "truth is in Jesus." Even at this early time the effort to drive a wedge between the Christ of faith and the Jesus of history was advocated, but this hodgepodge of heresy was soundly rejected in the early Church as it should be today. The heavenly Christ became Jesus, and the full truth about Christ is found in Jesus.

The new man (4:20-24). To become the new man, in contrast to the old man, a transformation takes place that is described with three infinitives: *apothesthai* (to put off), *ananeousthai* (to be renewed), and *endusasthai* (to put on). The new man is commanded to "put off (*apothesthai*, 4:22) that which belongs to his "former manner of life and is corrupt through deceitful lusts." This process of putting off includes the mortification of such sins of the flesh (II Cor. 7:1) as "immorality, impurity, passion, evil desire, and covetousness, which is idolatry" (Col. 3:5). Sins of the human spirit (II Cor. 7:1) must also be put away: "anger, wrath, malice, slander, and foul talk from your mouth" (Col. 3:8). The second step in becoming the new man is to be "renewed" (*ananeousthai*, 4:23). This renewal takes place in "the spirit" of the "mind." The human spirit is "the point of contact" in man with the Holy Spirit of God. Until there is union between man's spirit and God's Spirit, life is "corrupt through deceitful lusts." In darkness, alienation, and ignorance the mind becomes futile, emotions become frustrated, and the body becomes sensual. Only when the human spirit is in harmony with the Holy Spirit does the mind control the emotions and the desires of the body. The integration of the whole personality takes place when the spirit is renewed, for this is the pinnacle of personality and the point of contact with God. It is then that "the Spirit himself bears witness with our spirit that we are the children of God" (Rom. 8:16). To "be renewed in the spirit of your minds" is the regeneration of the whole life.

The third step in becoming the new man is "to put on" (*endusasthai*, 4:24). We are commanded to "put on the new man, that after God hath been created in righteousness and holiness of truth" (4:24, ASV). In the ancient baptismal liturgies the newly baptized person literally put on a white robe between his immersion and the reception at the Lord's Supper (Eucharist) immediately afterwards. Until this day one still hears the person receiving baptism called a "candidate," one who wears a white robe. The white robe was a symbol that "as many as were baptized into Christ have put on Christ" (Gal. 3:27). To put on Christ was to "put on the new man, that is being renewed unto knowledge after the image of him that created him" (Col. 3:10). The innocence of Paradise is restored.

The process of renewal begins at a point, as the three aorist infinitives indicate, but it is followed by a process. "Our inward man is renewed day by day" (II Cor. 4:16, ASV). One of the attractive features of the ancient baptismal liturgies is the fact that instruction, immersion, confirmation by the laying on of hands, and first communion were all parts of one service. Immersion in water as a confession of faith was no doubt a crucial moment, but there is much that goes before and much that follows after. The punctiliar fallacy that confines the work of the Holy Spirit to an underwater operation neglects the process of renewal that should begin before baptism and continue after baptism until the resurrection of the dead.

The Call to Walk in Love
(4:25-5:2)

It is not until the conclusion of this section that we are called to "walk in love" (5:2), but the six commandments before the conclusion call for the cessation of all things that are a contrast to love. Here is a splendid statement of what Thomas Chalmers called "the expulsive power of a new affection."'

The first commandment of love expels falsehood: "Therefore, putting away falsehood, let every one speak the truth with his neighbor, for we are members one of another" (4:25). The messianic hope had the command: "Speak the truth to one another, render in your gates judgments that are true and make peace" (Zech. 8:16). Now, as the powers of the messianic age are being manifest in the Church, the body of Christ, Christians are called to put away all falsehood in their relations for the profound reason that "we are members one of another." He who lies to his neighbor with whom he has this mutual relationship lies in part to himself.

One of the shocking signs of modern society is the assumption that only the naive tell the truth at all times. The "big lie" is a bad thing in politics, in fact one of the unstable factors in international relations, but things have sunk to a low ebb indeed when it is used to promote "the Lord's work." Why should truthfulness be some special virtue of the Quakers?

The second commandment of love calms anger: "Be angry but do not sin; do not let the sun go down on your anger, and give no place to the devil" (4:26f.). Psalm 4:4 says:

Be angry, but sin not;
commune with your own hearts
on your beds, and be silent.

The Pythagoreans said: "Do not let the sun go down on your anger." Love learns from both sources.

We are not commanded to get angry, as is often suggested, but to cool off quickly when we do. The Greek word for getting angry (*orgizomai*) means to get warm, and it will soon explode into sin if there is no cooling-off period to prevent it. When one opens his mouth in anger the devil is almost sure to step in, so keep your mouth shut and "give no opportunity to the devil."

A person once justified her anger by saying it was all over in a moment, but her anger was too much like an atom bomb that is followed by a deadly fallout and long radiation. In that moment the devil was given a wide opening. Even when no words are spoken anger can be too much like Tam O'Shanter's wife, "gathering her brow like a gathering storm, nursing her wrath to keep it warm."

The third commandment forbids stealing: "Let the thief no longer steal, but rather let him labor, doing honest work with his hands, so that he may be able to give to those in need" (4:28). For those coming out of pagan society, where stealing was often an ordinary means of livelihood, these were no idle words of instruction. Among the motley group washed in the waters of baptism by Paul were professional "thieves" (I Cor. 6:9-11), but he was not discouraged with their possibilities in honest Christian living.

Labor is a form of love, and the more one loves to labor the more it is a labor of love. Paul was not ashamed to say: "We labor, working with our own hands" (I Cor. 4:12). Who has not seen toil transformed by those who do even the most lowly labor as a service for God? Every person needs a form of employment for the good of his soul, and unemployment may soon become one of the most serious social problems.

Love is more fully expressed in labor when one is able to give the fruit of his honest work to help those in need. Even

"honest work" can lead to hardness if there is never an opportunity for generosity, but the earliest New Testament teachings are more severe on those who are always idle (I Thess.
4:11). To the lazy gluttons on the island of Crete the command is given: "And let our people learn to apply themselves
to good deeds, so as to help cases of urgent need, and not to
be unfruitful" (Tit. 3:14). A fruitful life is a full life, and a
full life is a labor of love.

The fourth commandment of love puts to silence evil talk:
"Let no evil talk come out of your mouths, but only such as
is good for edifying, as fits the occasion, that it may impart
grace to those who hear" (4:29). Speech, the power to communicate, is that mysterious power that makes a person. Personality may be defined as the power of self-communication,
or to enter into relation, and the misuse of this power in evil
talk is a perversion of personality.

As that mysterious power of self-communication, speech may
build and edify another person. The right word on the right
occasion, "as fits the occasion," makes good people as well as
a good society in which people are "able to communicate."
The failure to communicate destroys personality and disrupts
social relation. Who has not known the futility of shouting
across canyons at others?

Speech has power even to "impart grace to those who hear."
One often hears debate on whether sacraments, sacred signs,
can be "a means of grace" between God and man, but little is
said about the sounds of speech being a means by which grace
is imparted. In sign and sound, communion and conversation,
Christians may be edified and build the body of Christ in love.
It is this mysterious power that makes prophetic preaching
edification (I Cor. 14:1-5).

The fifth commandment of love warns against rebellion:
"And do not grieve the Holy Spirit of God, in whom you were
sealed for the day of redemption" (4:30). Behind this warning is the terrible example of those who perished in the wilderness even after they had been delivered from Egypt (Isa.
63:10):

But they rebelled
and grieved his holy Spirit;
therefore he turned to be their enemy,
and himself fought against them.

The sorrow of the Spirit is caused by rebellion against God. "A man who has violated the law of Moses dies without mercy at the testimony of two or three witnesses. How much worse punishment do you think will be deserved by the man who has spurned the Son of God, and profaned the blood of the covenant by which he was sanctified, and outraged the Spirit of grace?" (Heb. 10:28f.).

The seal of the Spirit points to the future, to "the day of redemption," not to the past, to the inheritance in the promised land, not to the fleshpots of Egypt. "In him you also, who have heard the word of truth, the gospel of your salvation, and have believed in him, were sealed with the promised Holy Spirit, which is the guarantee of our inheritance until we acquire possession of it, to the praise of his glory" (1:13f.). Let us not rebel and grieve his Holy Spirit.

The sixth commandment of love corrects the bad disposition: "Let all bitterness and wrath and anger and clamor and slander be put away from you, with all malice, and be kind to one another, tenderhearted, forgiving one another, as God in Christ forgave you" (14:31f.). "Anger, wrath, malice, slander" were listed in Colossians 3:8, but here "bitterness" and "clamor" have been added with "foul talk" omitted. The picture is the antithesis of love: anger (*thumos*, a passionate outburst), wrath (*orgē*, a settled feeling of anger), clamor (*kraugē*, shouting at one another), slander (*blasphēmia*, abusive language), malice (*kakia*, vicious disposition).

The three words that follow are intended to give the Christian contrast to this bad disposition. Kindness, tenderheartedness, and forgiveness describe the good disposition toward others. Kindness (*chrēstos*) means to be helpful, to lend a hand to one in need. It sounds so much like *Christos* (Christ) that the two words were often confused, and Tertullian comments on the confusion (*Apology*, V. 3, *Ad Nationes*, III).

The tenderhearted (*eusplagchnos,* merciful, goodhearted) are in contrast to the calloused and hardhearted who are past feeling (4:18f.). Forgiveness establishes a relationship between man and man that represents God's relation to man, literally, "gracing one another, as God in Christ graced you."

The grace of God in Christ creates a context for the conclusion: "Therefore be imitators of God, as beloved children. And walk in love as Christ loved us and gave himself up for us, a fragment offering and sacrifice to God" (5:1f.). It is difficult for those coming out of pagan society to grasp the meaning of the imitation of God. Often their gods had dispositions as bad as that which Christians are called upon to discard. Such imitation needs illustration.

The minor illustration is that of children (5:1). As little children tend to imitate their parents, so let the children of God, by words that "impart grace to those who hear," imitate God who imparted his grace to us in Christ. If God is our Father, we should live as children in his family.

The major illustration is that of Christ (5:2). In his sacrificial love he was both expiation and example, but here it is his example that is in view (cf. I Pet. 2:21). As the burnt offering of the Old Testament was "a pleasing odor, an offering by fire to the Lord" (Ex. 29:18), so the sacrifice of Christ was "a fragrant offering and sacrifice to God" (5:2). His love is the pattern for our personal relations in the family of God (cf. I Jno. 3:16). Nothing is said about love for our enemies (Mt. 5:43-48; Lk. 6:32-36), but this is not excluded. However, the place to start walking in love is in God's family.

THE CALL TO WALK IN THE LIGHT
(5:3-14)

The difference between pagan conduct and Christian is one of darkness and light. Paul, speaking of his Gentile mission, preached that he was sent "to open their eyes, that they may turn from darkness to light and from the power of Satan to God" (Acts 26:18). To the Christians of Colossae, where dwelt two thousand Jewish families transferred by Antiochus from Babylon, he wrote of God: "He has delivered us from the dominion of darkness and transferred us to the kingdom of his beloved Son, in whom we have redemption, the forgiveness of sins" (Col. 1:13f.).

This contrast between darkness and light became even stronger in the Johannine writings, mainly because pagan dualism penetrated into the Christian fellowship and led some to profess fellowship with Christ while they continued to walk in darkness (I Jno. 1:16). It is not uncommon even today to meet professed Christians who assume that the immoral deeds of the body do not damage the human spirit which is in fellowship with the Holy Spirit of God.

The sons of disobedience (5:3-6). Their present plight (5:3f.) is one of moral decay that must be denounced in order to walk in the light. Three words point up the perversity of their ways: "But immorality and all impurity or covetousness must not even be named among you, as is fitting among saints" (5:3). Immorality (*porneia*) and impurity (*akatharsia*) are immediately recognized as sexual offenses that contradict the Christian attitude toward the body. The body of the Christian, along with his spirit, is joined to the Lord, so it is a contradiction for him to join his body with a prostitute's (I Cor. 6:15). Such is the realism of Paul behind the present passages.

Covetousness (*pleonexia*) is not generally considered to be a term of sexual offense, but that is the meaning here (cf. 4:19). He who has sex relations with the wife of another defrauds him. In plain words Paul told the early converts from paganism: "This is the will of God, your sanctification: that you abstain from immorality; that each one of you know how to take a wife for himself in holiness and honor, not in the passion of lust like heathen who do not know God; that no man transgress, and wrong his brother in this matter, because the Lord is an avenger in all these things, as we solemnly forewarned you. For God has not called us for uncleanness, but in holiness. Therefore whoever disregards this, disregards not man but God, who gives his Holy Spirit to you" (I Thess. 4:3-8). The word "wrong" translates the infinitive *pleonektein,* from which the noun *pleonexia* (covetousness) comes.

Pagan deeds are such that Christian conversations do not mention them, for it is not "fitting among saints." These saints are no super-Christians, as popular opinion would think, but ordinary Christians seeking to live a life of moral purity. According to these moral standards many modern Christians live in a moral swamp.

Thanksgiving (*eucharistia*) comes in unexpectedly as a corrective to this pagan threat (5:4). It is not unreasonable to see in this word a suggestion of the Christian Eucharist, the breaking of the loaf and the drinking of the cup, which followed baptism from the earliest times (cf. I Cor. 10, 11). The Eucharist was a special occasion for the purging away of the leaven of pagan immorality (I Cor. 5). The second century only developed what was already a New Testament practice.[2]

If this is behind the moral instruction at this point, then the thanksgiving is a special theme that increases the significance of the statement: "Let there be no filthiness, nor silly talk, no levity, which are not fitting; but let there be thanksgiving" (5:4). There is more here than a general attitude of gratitude that directs Christian conversation. Participation in the body and blood of the Lord is no time to make a joke of indecency (cf. I Cor. 11:17-34). *Aischrotēs* (filthiness, baseness), *mōrologia* (silly talk, the speech of a fool), and *eutrapelia* (levity, facetiousness) express this reduction of Christian morality to a big joke.

The future of the sons of disobedience (5:5f.) is no better than their present plight. It is the will of God that their future be the "inheritance in the kingdom of Christ and of God" (5:5), but this will never be if pagan morals are not left behind. "Be sure of this, that no immoral or impure man, or one who is covetous [that is, an idolater], has any inheri-

---

[2] E. C. Whitaker, *Documents of the Baptismal Liturgy,* pp. 1-7, etc.

tance in the kingdom of Christ and of God" (5:5). These are the same three words seen in 5:3, but this time covetousness is more clearly defined. It is far more than the failure to pledge a tithe on budget Sunday; it means here to make the house of God the house of prostitution, the common practice in pagan religion.

Our present participation in the kingdom began when God "delivered us from the dominion of darkness and transferred us to the kingdom of his beloved Son, in whom we have redemption, the forgiveness of sins" (Col. 1:13f.), but the "inheritance in the kingdom of Christ and of God" is yet future. *Klēronomia* (inheritance) has the same meaning here as it does in Ephesians 1:14 (man's) and 1:18 (God's). The powers of the kingdom are now present, but the glory of the kingdom is yet future.[3] It is "the kingdom of Christ and of God" because it was given to Christ by God at his exaltation and will be given back to God in the consummation, "the great abdication" (cf. I Cor. 15:23f.).

The wrath of God, not the kingdom of God, is in the future for those who practice pagan morals. "Let no one deceive you with empty words, for it is because of these things that the wrath of God comes upon the sons of disobedience" (5:6). Much preaching today is no more than deception and empty words, for immorality is covered rather than confessed, justified rather than rebuked. The wrath of God too is experienced in the present process of moral retribution (Rom. 1:18), but here, as with the kingdom, it is future, "the day of wrath when God's righteous judgment shall be revealed" (Rom. 2:5).

Those who disobey God's moral law are "the sons of disobedience," and it is deception to tell them that they will inherit God's kingdom. "Do not be deceived; neither the immoral, nor idolaters, nor adulterers, nor homosexuals, nor thieves, nor the greedy, nor drunkards, nor revilers, nor robbers will inherit the kingdom of God" (I Cor. 6:9f.). Men

[3] See my book *The Hope of Glory*, ch. 5.

need words that "impart grace to those who hear" (4:29), not "empty words" (*kenoi logoi*) that deceive.

The children of light (5:7-14). In the light life is fruitful (5:7-10), in contrast to the "unfruitful works of darkness" (5:11). "Therefore do not associate with them, for once you were darkness, but now you are light in the Lord; walk as children of light (for the fruit of light is found in all that is good and right and true), and try to learn what is pleasing to the Lord" (5:7-10). Two matters of translation and text require comment. The genitive *autōn* (RSV "with them") is better translated "in them," i.e., in the deeds of the sons of disobedience rather than with the persons. The dative is used of persons. Then some texts speak of "the fruit of the Spirit" (KJV), assimilating this from Galatians 5:22, but the better text is "the fruit of the light" (RSV).

This life of light is first of all a transformed life (5:8f.). The transformation of the relation to God ("at one time . . . but now, 2:11, 13) has now become a transformation in conduct ("once — now," 5:8). Christian conduct is summarized in a powerful parenthesis "(for the fruit of light is found in all that is good and right and true)" (5:9). There is no part of life that is not transformed by the light (cf. I John 1:5-7; 2:8-11; John 3:19-21), and the daily life is a demonstration in morals ("walk," "fruit").

This life of light is also a tested life (5:10). Moral discrimination tries "to learn what is pleasing to the Lord" and to live in this new light. All is laid on the altar to "prove what is the will of God, what is good and acceptable and perfect" (Rom. 12:2). Such children "shine as lights in the world" (Phil. 2:15).

In the darkness life is unfruitful (5:11-13). These "unfruitful works of darkness" (cf. *autōn*, 5:7) should be shunned. The good life does not grow in darkness. "But you are not in darkness, brethren, for that day to surprise you like a thief. For you are sons of the day; we are not of the night nor of darkness. So then let us not sleep as others do, but let us keep awake and be sober. For those who sleep sleep at night, and those who get drunk get drunk at night" (I Thess. 5:5-7). The works of darkness are really a shame (5:12f.). In secret societies even religious rites are a practice of immoralities. Only the light of a good life can expose the fallacy of pagan teaching and the unfruitfulness of such a life. The life that is "made manifest" (*phaneroumenon*, passive participle), not "becomes manifest" (RSV), is the life of light. Life is transformed by turning light on the darkness.

Many suggestions have been made as to the source of the quotation which comes as a conclusion to this paragraph (5:14):

Awake, O sleeper, and rise from the dead,
and Christ shall give you light.

It is generally thought to be a Christian baptismal hymn built on certain Old Testament passages (Isa. 60:1; 9:2, etc. Cf. Eph. 4:8).

Strong support for this suggestion may be found in a similar hymn in Romans 13:11-14, ASV:

Already it is time for you
to awake from sleep:
for now is salvation nearer to us
than when we first believed.

The night is far spent,
the day is at hand:
let us therefore cast off the works of darkness,
and let us put on the armor of light.

Let us walk becomingly,
as in the day;
not in revelling and drunkenness,
not in chambering and wantonness,
not in strife and jealousy.

But put ye on the Lord Jesus Christ,
and make not provision
for the flesh,
(*to fulfill* the lusts *thereof*).

In the ancient baptismal liturgies this passage from darkness to light was elaborated in the words by which Satan was renounced and by which adherence to Christ was declared. One of the best illustrations appears in *The Mystagogical Catecheses* of Cyril of Jerusalem, about A.D. 350. To these who had passed through the waters of baptism and were now qualified to participate in the Eucharist, it was said (1:4):

> However, thou are bidden with arm outstretched to say to him as though actually present, I RENOUNCE THEE SATAN.
> I wish to say, wherefore ye stand facing to the West; for it is necessary. Since the West is the region of sensible darkness, and he being darkness, has his dominion also in darkness, ye therefore, looking with a symbolical meaning toward the West, renounce that dark and gloomy potentate.[4]

THE CALL TO WALK CAREFULLY
(5:15-20)

The KJV ("that ye walk circumspectly") is about as well supported in the manuscript evidence as the RSV ("look carefully"), but the meaning is also about the same. A careful walk requires knowledge both of the will and the worship of God.

Wisdom (5:15-17). Knowledge of the will of God is wisdom. It is unwise to waste our time doing that which is inconsistent with the faith which we profess, for time is of the essence in our witness to the world. "Conduct yourselves wisely toward outsiders, making the most of time" (Col. 4:5). Stewardship of time is as important as stewardship of possessions, and it is one thing that all have in common. As long as we live together in this world, one has as much time as the other; it really depends on how we use the time that all have in common.

The sanctification of time by special periods for private prayer and gathering together in public prayer is certainly no waste of time. Neglect of these special seasons for spiritual

[4] F. L. Cross, ed., *St. Cyril of Jerusalem's Lectures on the Christian Sacraments*, pp. 54f.

renewal will secularize the whole of life, as any realistic reflection reveals. We are indeed not called to be a calendar cult that judges with "regard to a festival or a new moon or a sabbath" (Col. 2:16), but let us not neglect "to meet together, as is the habit of some, and all the more as you see the Day drawing near" (Heb. 10:25).

This positive emphasis on precious time is prompted by the evil of our days ("because the days are evil," 5:16). Why should Christians fritter away time when the world around us works overtime for evil? If one calls for a period of fasting and prayer as a remedy for the evil of our time, even some church members view it as naive and eccentric, but if the night is spent in drunkenness and immorality it is brushed aside as "the thing everybody does."

An understanding of "what the will of the Lord is" (5:17) overcomes the foolish frittering away of time. It is sad to see people moving toward the end of their expected years still uncertain as to what the meaning of their lives can be, but there is great joy in that youth who early discerns what work God wants him or her to do. This pertains not only to the major missions of life but to the new tasks of each new day.

Worship (5:18-20). The worship of God is the way to discern the will of God. Pagan religion in the cult of Dionysus developed the attitude that salvation (*sōtēria*) is debauchery (*asōtia*), release from inhibited feelings by intoxication, deliverance from depression by debauchery. Many a modern person who never heard of Dionysus lives by this rule. Even the more ethical Epicurean gets it off his chest with "Let us eat and drink, for tomorrow we die" (I Cor. 15:32).

Some of this spirit of sensuality was almost sure to be brought into the life of the Church, as drunkenness at the Lord's Supper in Corinth indicates. Hans Lietzmann, in his famous work on *The Mass and Lord's Supper*,[5] concluded that there were two different celebrations in the primitive church. One he called the Jerusalem type, a remembrance of the table

[5] See Bibliography.

fellowship that the disciples had with the Lord in the days of his flesh and an anticipation of the messianic banquet in the coming kingdom of God. References in Acts to the breaking of bread (2:42, 46; 20:11, cf. 16:34; Lk. 24:30, 35), with no mention of the cup, are thought to reflect this practice. The Pauline type included the common cup (I Cor. 10:16f.; 11: 17-34).

In a brilliant essay[6] Oscar Cullmann has taken up the problem afresh and brought it very near to solution. Against the background of the researches of Lietzmann and Cullmann, it is possible that the Lord's Supper mentioned in I Corinthians 11:17-34 was a combination of what came to be called the love-feast (*agapē*, Jude 12) and the Last Supper. Before the breaking of the loaf and the drinking of the cup (11:23-26; 10:16f.), the love-feast opened the way for Dionysian excesses (11:17-22). After the separation of the two, due partly to Paul's rebukes, the second part of the service came to be called the Eucharist (from *eucharisteō*, "I give thanks) (11:24, cf. 14:16f.), a term found frequently in the early Church (*Didache*, 9:1; Ignatius, *Philad.* 4; Justin, *Apology*, I.66; etc.).

If this be behind Ephesians 5:18-20, as *eucharistountes* (giving thanks) in 5:20 would suggest, there is more here than a general attitude of gratitude. The thought has moved from baptism, which the baptismal hymn in 5:14 and much of the instruction in 5:3-14 fit, to a celebration given briefly in 5:18-20 that is very similar to the details found in I Corinthians 11:17-34. The more one ponders the whole Ephesian letter the more the pattern of public worship appears.

The fulness of the Spirit is the Christian corrective to Dionysian drunkenness. Today, as at Pentecost, the worship and witness of those filled with the Holy Spirit is most likely to meet the mock: "These are filled with new wine" (Acts 2:12). Unfortunately some congregations have more of the atmosphere of being drugged than being drunk, of stagnation than

---

[6] Oscar Cullmann and F. J. Leenhardt, *Essays on the Lord's Supper*, pp. 5-23.

intoxication. One really wonders how many of our "established churches" would react to the situation described in some detail in I Corinthians 14. It is good to know that one denomination is reacting in the right way, at least in some quarters.[7]

The melody of people "filled with the Spirit, addressing one another in psalms and hymns and spiritual songs" (5:18f.) is a major need now as then. Already it has been pointed out that here is the Holy Trinity in hymnology. Psalms in praise of God (especially the so-called Hallel Psalms, 113-118) sung at the Passover became a central part of the early Christian worship. In the house churches and in the synagogue churches these took on deeper meaning in God's salvation history. For hundreds of years the later churches would sing Psalm 42 on the way to baptism and Psalm 23 as the newly baptized returned to participate in the Eucharist for the first time. Pliny the Younger (c. A.D. 112) reported to the Emperor Trajan that Christians "were accustomed on a fixed day to gather before daybreak and to sing antiphonally a hymn to Christ as to a god" (*Letters* X.96).

It is often suggested that this may be a reference to the majestic hymn included in John 1:1-18 (1-5, 10f., 14, 18).[8] More than a score of hymns, as the Moffatt translation notes, are quoted in part or as a whole in I Corinthians alone. Romans 5:12-21, 6:3-11, 8:31-38, 13:11-14 may be completed hymns, and Revelation rings with the praise of the redeemed. Philippians 2:5-11, I Peter 3:18-22, I Timothy 3:16, 6:1f., II Timothy 1:9f., 2:11-13, Titus 2:11-14, 3:4-7 are all hymns.[9] How the New Testament Christians sang the praises of Christ! Spiritual songs were sung in the Spirit, making the Trinity complete.

This high hymnology is matched by a high christology. "Let

---

[7] *The Living Church*, January, 1961.

[8] Humphrey C. Green, "The Composition of St. John's Prologue," *The Expository Times*, LXVI (1955), 291-294.

[9] Many have been put to music by J. C. Wansey, *New Testament Psalter*.

the word of Christ dwell in you richly, as you teach and admonish one another in all wisdom, and as you sing psalms and hymns and spiritual songs with thankfulness in your hearts to God" (Col. 3:16). In Colossians 3:16 they sing "to God," but with difficulty. Ephesians 5:19 says to sing "to the Lord," and Lord seems almost sure to mean "our Lord Jesus Christ" (5:20; cf. 5:8, 10, 17, 19). Here is real Christianity, the type too often toned down today.

Chapter Five:

THE CHRISTIAN HOUSEHOLD
(5:21-6:9)

It is difficult to imagine a weaker point in the message and method of the modern Church than in the neglect of the Christian household. At the very point where, despite the problems of a pagan culture, the early Church was strong and successful we are threatened with failure under the pressures of secular society. More and more one sees that neither individualism nor collectivism in the Church can cope with the present challenge. Perhaps a return from the church house to the house church will help.

Already the place of the house church has been mentioned (I Cor. 16:19; Col. 4:15; Phile. 2; Rom. 16:5), and the meaning of household baptisms has turned attention to this unit of social solidarity (Acts 16:15, 34; 18:8; I Cor. 1:16). The relations of a Christian household, both within and without, offer much hope for our time. In I Peter both the outward relations of Christian citizenship (2:11-17) and the inward relations of the Christian household (2:18-3:7) occupy a prominent position and are regulated by submission as seen in the obedience of the servant of the Lord and his fulfilment in the sufferings of Christ. In Ephesians 5:21-6:9, building as it does on the special problem of slavery as it appears in Colossians 3:18-4:1, these social relations that confronted the Christian household are surveyed in the light of reverence for Christ.

This ethical principle of reverence for Christ (5:21) has many expressions in the New Testament faith (cf. Mt. 25:31-46; I Pet. 2:13; Col. 3:18), but the concept of the Church as the body of Christ offers the best possible background for comprehensive understanding. One is to relate himself to a member of Christ's mystical body as he would relate himself to Christ in the flesh, and the chief concern of personal rights is transformed into a relation of mutual reverence for personal human beings.

Justice, which raises the question of human rights, ruled the best in Roman society. Plato's great vision in the *Republic* grouped those of a just society according to the cardinal virtues: workmen, representing temperance; soldiers, fortitude; and the philosophers, wisdom. With all of these working in harmony a society of justice can be maintained. To-day's social chaos makes even this vision look desirable.

Yet there is a greater vision than justice. Augustine almost drew a plan for this society when he wrote his *City of God* in the crumbling ruins of Plato's *Republic*. The Bishop of Hippo saw a drama of two cities in history, one the city of earth in which men love themselves until they have contempt for God, and the other the city of God where men love God until they have contempt for themselves (*City of God*, XIV.28). This was the basis of a medieval society that has much to offer to a contemporary society threatened with destruction.

But we would not be able to return to the Middle Ages if we tried. Modern men must dream their own dreams and see their own visions if a creative society based on Christian principles is to be even partly realized before the riddles of all history are disclosed in the consummation of the ages. If the creative society comes out of our present chaos it will be when Christians shake off the skeptical cynicism of so much current talk and become completely committed to the Church as the one body of Christ in which men live in mutual relation "out of reverence for Christ."

WIVES AND HUSBANDS
(5:21-24)

Wives (5:21-24). Reverence for Christ is the rule that should regulate all human relations in the body of Christ, the Church: "Be subject to one another out of reverence for Christ" (5:21). It is important to note this broader application of mutual submission of all Christians lest the specific regulations be thought of in terms of tyranny and subjugation.

The standard of submission for the Christian wife appeals to the role of "the Lord" and the "head." It is less difficult to submit to the husband "as to the Lord" (5:22) when both are Christians, but I Peter 3:1f. applies the principle even in homes where the husband does "not obey the word." Sarah, in her obedience and submission to Abraham when she called him "Lord," is the example for the Christian wife.

Appeal to the husband as "head of the wife as Christ is the head of the church" strengthens the order of creation with the order of redemption. The submission of the Christian wife belongs to a series of sacred submissions that culminate in the relation of Christ to God: "the head of every man is Christ, the head of a woman is her husband, and the head of Christ is God." (I Cor. 11:3). That is why it is "fitting in the Lord" (Col. 3:18). As Christ protects and provides for the Church as its Savior, so the Christian husband is the head of the wife.

The scope of submission for the Christian wife includes "everything." As the Church should be completely submissive to Christ, so Christian wives should "be subject in everything to their husbands" (5:24). It is not the subjugation of woman but the imitation of Christ that guides the thought here, and it is unfortunate when these verses are used to justify domination rather than to encourage devotion. The modern emancipation of woman, like the emancipation of slaves, is a logical outcome of the Christian gospel, but disaster develops when devotion to husband and home is destroyed. Much of the emotional and social instability of the modern

home is due to the destruction of this devotion. A devoted
wife is the strength of a home.

Husbands (5:25-33). Husbands are taught to love their
wives. The subjection of the wife to her husband has the
love of the husband for the wife as a corollary. Once when
the title for an expository sermon was submitted to a director
of publicity as "Husbands Love Your Wives" it was not printed
because it was assumed to be a joke. No preacher would
think of preaching on that topic!

The command for the husband to love his wife is twofold.
He is first to love his wife as "Christ loved the church." "Husbands, love your wives, as Christ loved the church and gave
himself up for her, that he might sanctify her, having cleansed
her by the washing of water with the word, that the church
might be presented before him in splendor, without spot or
wrinkle or any such thing, that she might be holy and without
blemish" (5:25-27).

If the husband loves his wife as Christ loved the Church
it will be a love that is sacrificial. It cost Christ to love the
Church. Self-sacrifice is the very essence of love. There
is a type of sexual love (*erōs*) that Plato, in his *Symposium*,
displays as both earthly and heavenly, and this is no doubt
a very important factor in the relationship between husband
and wife. To suppress this or leave it out of consideration
only distorts the relation. It is necessary also to take into
consideration the social love (*philia*) which is expressed in
the friendship that should exist between those bound in wed-
lock, and disastrous emotional problems arise when the relation does not include this factor. The highest form of love
(*agapē*) is sacrificial love, and this does not exclude the other
forms. The higher includes and fulfils the lower forms of love.

Erōs and *philia* can be understood by the many sexual and
social examples that are normal for human experience, but
the sacrificial love is most perfectly demonstrated in the self-
sacrifice of our Lord. Behind the sacrificial love by which
Christ gave himself for the corporate group of the Church
stands the personal experience by which Paul was crucified

with Christ. "I have been crucified with Christ; it is no longer I who live, but Christ who lives in me; and the life I now live in the flesh I live by faith in the Son of God, who loved me and gave himself for me" (Gal. 2:20). It is this sacrificial love that rightly relates the husband to the wife.

The love that Christ had for the Church was not only sacrificial; it was a love that led to sanctification. It was the purpose of Christ, when he gave himself for the Church, "that he might sanctify her, having cleansed her by the washing of water with the word, that the church might be presented before him in splendor, without spot or wrinkle or any such thing, that she might be holy and without blemish" (5:27). It is this process of sanctification that is so vitally related to our Lord's sacrificial love.

Sanctification is at times described as a point in the past when the transformation of sinful men begins to give way to the holiness of God. This point at which the process began marks the great discontinuity with pagan morals. "But such were some of you. But you were washed, you were sanctified, you were justified in the name of the Lord Jesus and in the Spirit of our God" (I Cor. 6:11). The three aorist tenses (washed, sanctified, justified) indicated that all of these benefits began at the same time. Sanctification is also a present process that continues as long as we "cleanse ourselves from every defilement of body and spirit, and make holiness perfect in the fear of God" (II Cor. 7:1). The future perfection of sanctification is the last stage in the process, and this is the view in mind in Ephesians 5:26.

Cleansing puts the emphasis on the past in Ephesians 5:26, but this also is repeated in some measure in the Christian life. The crisis of catharsis (Greek, *katharisas*) is followed by continuous cleansing. This is most clearly taught in the Johannine writings: "Every branch in me that beareth not fruit, he taketh it away: and every branch that beareth fruit, he cleanseth (*katharei*) it, that it may bear more fruit. Already ye are clean (*katharoi*) because of the word which

I have spoken unto you" (John 15:2f., ASV). Spiritual catharsis cleanses the Christian life to make it fruitful.

Washing is a third way to describe the process of sanctification. In I Corinthians 6:11 washing and sanctification are closely linked with justification, and all three mark the beginning of the new life in Christ. This washing is associated with baptism in some places, and that is perhaps the case here. "Rise and be baptized, and wash away your sins, calling on his name" (Acts 22:16). There is no automatic relation between baptism and the forgiveness of sins, but this is certainly the normal association with the act of washing (cf. Mk. 1:4; Acts 2:38).

The relationship between the water and the word has led to several views. Some would see this as the *cleansing* word. The word is the water which cleanses from sin. "You are already made clean by the word which I have spoken to you" (John 3:5). Some support can be found for this in the Rabbinic sources that compare the Torah to water, but it does not seem sufficient to identify water and word.[1]

Others think of the *creative* word. As the word brought life into being in the watery chaos of the original creation (Gen. 1:1-3), so the word of God pronounced over the candidate cleanses from sin and imparts the new life. The theologians of the Greek churches gave this as an unusual interpretation, and similar ideas may be suggested by Tertullian's use of Genesis I in interpreting baptism (*De Baptismo,* 4).

A third approach may be called the *confessional* word, and that seems most probable. This would interpret *en hrēmati* (with the word) to have reference to the confession made by the candidate in his baptism. It is the word "on your lip and in your heart (that is, the word of faith which we preach)" when "you confess with your lips that Jesus is Lord and believe in your heart that God raised him from the dead" (Rom. 10:8f.). If this be correct, the passage is of great importance

---

[1] E. K. Lee, *The Religious Thought of St. John,* pp. 216-219.

in understanding believer's baptism. Even immersion is not baptism without the confession of Jesus Christ as Lord.

The presentation of the Church in splendor (*endoxon*) is a picture in which Christ as bridegroom both prepares and presents the bride "to himself" (KJV). Out of the process of sanctification, cleansing, and washing, comes the Church as a pure bride. "I feel a divine jealousy for you, for I betrothed you to Christ to present you as a pure bride to her one husband" (II Cor. 11:2). In this passage Paul betroths and presents the Church to Christ, but the presentation in Ephesians 5:27 is by Christ himself. The splendor signifies the appearance of Christ. "When Christ who is our life appears, then you also will appear with him in glory" (Col. 3:4).

The spotless state (*mē echousan spilon*) is a future one in which all the stains of sin have been removed from the white robe of the bride of Christ. In the ancient love feasts, which preceded the Eucharist in the Lord's Supper, there was always the danger of spots (*spilades*), and this would leave blemishes on the brotherhood (Jude 12). "They are blots and blemishes, reveling in their dissipation, carousing with you" (II Pet. 2:13). In the process of sanctification these are all removed, and the bride of Christ appears spotless.

The wrinkle (*hrutida*) of old age does not disfigure the bride of Christ. In glory it will not be as it was with Hosea, whose wife Gomer went with strange lovers until she was a withered and wrinkled old woman, or with the Lord when Israel left her bridegroom and went off to worship the Baals. As a bride that never grows old so the Church will be enveloped in glory with Christ her bridegroom. That will be the new Jerusalem that comes down out of heaven "as a bride adorned for her husband" (Rev. 21:2).

The holy bonds of sacrificial love will in the end make for the holy estate, the end of the process of sanctification. To describe this state as "holy and without blemish" (*hagia kai amōmos*) is to return to the ultimate purpose of God (1:4). The very term is a sacrificial one, and it is through sacrificial love, "as Christ loved the church and gave himself up for her" (5:25), that the blemishes are removed.

Seven words have been used to describe the outcome of Christ's sacrificial love: "sanctify . . . cleansed . . . washing . . . splendor . . . without spot or wrinkle . . . holy and without blemish." "Sanctify" (hagiasē) and "holy" (hagia) are considered one, the noun being the final state of the verb.

It is generally thought that this is a baptismal passage, and no good reason appears for rejecting this interpretation. Baptism is the outward sign of the inward washing that takes place when belief and baptism are brought together. The practice of baptism without belief on the part of the recipient, even when such baptism is performed in the believing congregation for the infant of believing parents, fails to do justice to New Testament baptism. The Church has put asunder what Christ joined together.

Even so it is the spiritual significance that is central. One may be inwardly cleansed without the outward washing, provided his lack of baptism is not wilful disobedience to what he recognizes as the command of Christ, and it is this washing that is true regeneration. However, it is a pity that the picture is so distorted by a severance of the sign from the spiritual experience.

Washing alone is not all there is to the process of sanctification. Frequent cleansing is also needed (Jno. 13:10). The prayer of William L. Stidger is ever needed:

> *I saw God wash the world last night*
> *With his sweet showers on high,*
> *And then, when morning came, I saw*
> *Him hang it out to dry.*
>
> *He washed each tiny blade of grass*
> *And every trembling tree;*
> *He flung his showers against the hill,*
> *And swept the billowing sea.*
>
> *The white rose is a cleaner white,*
> *The red rose is more red,*

Since God washed every fragrant face
And put them all to bed.

There's not a bird, there's not a bee
That wings along the way
But is a cleaner bird and bee
Than it was yesterday.

I saw God wash the world last night.
Ah, would He had washed me
As clean of all my dust and dirt
As that old white birch tree.[2]

In the second step husbands are told to love their wives as their own bodies (5:28). Moving from the sacrificial love of Christ to self-love incorporates an important corrective to much modern thought. The love of man for himself is not the great sin giving rise to all sin; it is, rather, that self-love which refuses to love others as it loves itself. Alienation and exclusion from others in our self-love is the original sin.

When the husband loves his life as he loves himself, it will always be a love that cares. "Even so husbands should love their wives as their own bodies. He who loves his wife loves himself. For no man ever hates his own flesh, but nourishes and cherishes it, as Christ does the church, because we are members of his body" (5:28-30). After the tendency to turn from the Church as the body of Christ to the Church as the bride of Christ, the discussion returns to the metaphor of the body with even greater realism.

Love of man for himself is assumed but not condemned. On this assumption the husband is to recognize his wife as a part of his selfhood. If the husband is the wife's head, the wife is the husband's body! This union of selfhood in marriage is both physical and spiritual. Sexual union alone makes the wife a part of the husband's personality. The best commentary on this vital union is to be found in I Corinthians 6:15-20. In protest to the pagan practice of prostitution Paul asks a question with a penetrating comment: "Know ye not that he that

---

[2] James Dalton Morrison, ed., *Masterpieces of Religious Verse*, p. 14.

is joined (*ho kollōmenos*) to a harlot is one body? . . . But he that is joined (*ho de kollōmenos*) unto the Lord is one spirit" (I Cor. 6:16f., ASV). How can he use the same word for the union of a man with a prostitute that he uses for the union of a Christian with Christ? It is because even the prostitute becomes part of the selfhood of the man who is "joined" to her body.

If this be true in lust, and much modern promiscuity ignores this truth, then how much more is it true in love. Man is a living soul who has a human body and a human spirit. His human body is part of his very soul, the part with which he joins himself to the physical world, and his human spirit is that with which he joins himself to the Holy Spirit and thus to Christ. Therefore, sexual union between husband and wife makes the wife a part of the very soul of the husband, and his soul is himself.

The loss that a husband feels on the death of his wife, or even in prolonged absence from her, is evidence for the profound truth of this view of marriage. When the husband loses his wife he loses a part of his very selfhood. It is even a greater loss than the loss of an eye, an arm, or a leg, for the wife is a person, far more than an organ, who belongs to his selfhood. He who has heard with sympathy the words of loneliness lingering in the heart of a bereaved husband or who has some experience of long absence from his wife will not need to know the Greek words to grasp the truth of this teaching!

Spiritual union is even higher than sexual union. Indeed, sexual union without spiritual union, a union of human bodies without union of human spirits, is immoral and leads to a sense of guilt and frustration. In revolt against this sordid view of sex, some early Christians practiced what has been called spiritual marriage, spiritual companionship in Christian service without physical marriage in sexual union. The translation of I Corinthians 7:36-38 in the RSV assumes this to be the case in Corinth, and it is sure that it became the practice of some moral athletes in the second century (*Herm.*

Sim. IX, 11:1-4). All of this indicates the high view of the man and woman relation with which the early Christians made their protest against pagan promiscuity.

The relation between husband and wife now deepens into the relation of Christ to the Church. It is as though the Christian household has for the moment been swallowed up in the household of God. What started as a discussion of a human relation has soared all of a sudden into a divine relation. "For no man ever hates his own flesh, but nourishes and cherishes it, as Christ does the church, because we are members of his body" (5:29f.). He who loves his wife as he loves himself will love her as Christ loves the Church, for the wife belongs to the body of her husband as Christians belong to the body of Christ.

The members of the body of Christ were discussed by Paul in I Corinthians 12:1-31 in relation to spiritual gifts. The varieties of spiritual gifts (12:4-11) are unified by their proper use in the one body of Christ (12:12-26), and this forms the basis for order in the spiritual organism which is the true Church (12:27-31). Each member is nourished and cherished by Christ as a part of his body, and the Christian husband is called to have the same care for his wife.

The love that cares is the love that also cleaves (5:31). In the creation story man is constituted as a soul; living dust in relation to the dust of the ground (Gen. 2:4-9), a servant in relation to God (2:10-17), and a society in relation to his wife (2:18-24). At no place is the concept of social solidarity better illustrated than in God's intention for man and woman: "Therefore a man leaves his father and his mother and cleaves to his wife, and they become one flesh" (2:24). It is this oneness of man and woman that makes all severance of the marriage relation a serious disruption of the created order, and it is love for the wife as love for one's own self that avoids this severance of selfhood.

The marriage relation has profound significance. It is not only significant for understanding human selfhood, but it is also a type of Christ's sacred marriage to the Church. The

ASV is translated much nearer the Greek than the KJV and the RSV: "This mystery is great, but I speak in regard of Christ and the church" (5:32). The Latin Vulgate of Jerome translates *musterion* (mystery) as *sacramentum* (sacrament). This became the basis for belief in marriage as one of the seven sacraments, but even Roman Catholic scholars today recognize this as incorrect.

The human marriage is a mystery because it is a type of the higher truth of a mystical marriage between Christ and the Church. This mystical relation between the Lord and Israel was a major factor in the covenant theology of the Old Testament. The immoral associations of the idea in Baalism were a factor in Hosea's prophecy that a day would come when it would be modified: "And it shall be at that day, saith the LORD, that thou shalt call me Ishi; and shalt call me no more Baali" (2:16). *Ishi* means my man, and *Baali* means my master, but Baali continued to be used to describe the relation between the Lord and Israel. Even the great chapter in Jeremiah on the new covenant speaks of "my covenant which they broke, though I was their husband [*Baal*], says the LORD" (31:32). And again: "For your maker is your husband [*Baal*], the LORD of hosts is his name" (Isa. 54:5).

It is this idea of holy marriage that leads to the mystical and mysterious concept of Christ in relation to the Church. As there is only one body of Christ, so there is only one bride of Christ, for Christ is no polygamist. He is the faithful bridegroom, and the Church is called to be his faithful bride (II Cor. 11:2; cf. Mk. 2:19f.).

After this lofty flight into the mysterious relation between Christ and the Church, the discussion on the relation between husband and wife returns to the second standard for the husband's love: "however, let each one of you love his wife as himself, and let the wife see that she respects her husband" (5:33). The mutual relation of love and respect (reverence) summarizes the main ideas that underlie the Christian view of husband and wife.

At no time in Christian history has the sanctity of the husband-wife relation been more threatened than at the present. Anxiety grips the hearts of members of the church when homes within the household of faith are shattered for lack of that social solidarity that belongs to both the good order of creation and the redemptive order of grace. The severance of husband and wife before death is a contradiction of the very intention of God in his creation of man (Mk. 10:1-9; Mt. 29:1-9).

CHILDREN AND PARENTS
(6:1-4)

Children (6:1-3). It is a moral obligation for Christian children to obey their Christian parents. This assumes, of course, that the commands of the parents will not be in conflict with the commands of Christ. "Children, obey your parents in the Lord, for this is right" (6:1). The phrase "in the Lord," already met in other connections (4:1, 17), has reference to that mystical union of Christians with Christ, and the moral relation of Christian children with their Christian parents to be regulated by this spiritual relationship shared by all members of a Christian household.

Appeal is first made to the right (6:1). Child psychology has increased our knowledge of how important it is for children to learn what is right long before their adolescent years bring the stress and strain between puberty and maturity. Parents, playmates, and heroes shape their characters, but the greatest of these is parents. It is therefore very important for parents to provide the true standard of right for the child.

It may seem queer to return to the question of Christian baptism in this connection, and indeed it is, but the consideration of the Ephesian letter as a baptismal document, as all the previous discussion presupposes, has been used as New Testament evidence for infant baptism.

> In the fifth chapter St. Paul speaks of the Christian family and Christian marriage in the context of the Church as the Body of Christ, and goes on immediately in the sixth chapter

to address children within the same Body, it being taken
for granted that they are members of Christ's Body, of his
flesh and of his bones. For children to be among the *saints,*
the *faithful,* the members of the Body of Christ, would be
quite unthinkable in the New Testament unless they were
baptized.[3]

Baptists should read such statements with patience, for if
our opposition to infant baptism has been an error it should
be corrected in the interest of both truth and Christian unity,
but this type of exposition is hard to receive as correct. It is
true that the later liturgies spoke only of the baptized as "the
faithful" and that Titus 1:6 speaks of "faithful children"
(*tekna echōn pista*), but how does one derive infant baptism
from this? The passage in Titus 1:6 says that the presbyter
(elder) must be "the husband of one wife, having children
that believe, who are not accused of riot or unruly." It
plainly says that they are "children that believe," and is one
able to imagine infants being "accused of riot or unruly"
(*asōtias ē anupotakta*)? An infant in drunken debauchery, for
asōtia is so used in Ephesians 5:18, and creating disorder
would indeed be a holy terror! Yet the above quote is followed by appeal to this passage.

All children born into a Christian household, even when
only one parent is Christian, are holy (I Cor. 7:14). To say
that this holiness is derived from baptism is consistent only
when one is willing to go on and insist that the holiness of
the unbelieving husband is also drived from his baptism, but
this no one is prepared to defend. The holiness of the husband like that of the child is derived from the holy woman,
the Christian saint, to whom both are physically related. This
holy husband is not saved by virtue of this holiness (cf.
I Cor. 7:16), and the passage does not mean that the child
will not need to believe and be baptized later to complete
his relationship to Christ. Until he reaches the age of responsibility he is a Christian child and should be so con-

[3] *Interim Report of the Special Commission on Baptism,* The Church
of Scotland, May, 1955, p. 26.

sidered, but this is no proof of his baptism. Birth makes him a Christian child until he rejects that into which he was born. After appeal to the right, a further appeal is made to promise (6:2f.). The primacy of the fifth commandment for children in relation to their parents is indicated by "first." It is the only one of the Ten Commandments with a promise, but the primacy is seen in the place of importance which it occupies in the Christian household. Solidarity has one of its most solid supports in the commandment: "Honor your father and mother." This was true in the society of Israel (Ex. 20:12; Deut. 5:16), and to some degree it is true in the Confucianism of China. It is well that ancient Christians incorporated this teaching found in the Old Testament, and missionary theology would do well to do the same with the sense of filial loyalty in oriental society. The stability of both church and state rest on this foundation in the family circle.

The promise of the fifth commandment reflects the Old Testament view of life. Earthly life in the promised land, filled with the quality of goodness and blessed with longevity, was the major hope in the national eschatology of Israel. As the hope for the nation waned, the hope for the individual increased, but it was not until the New Testament times that eternal life, both here and hereafter, came into full focus.[4] This hope of an earthly life ("that it may be well with you and that you may live long on the earth") is not discarded by the prominence of hope in eternal life, for "godliness is of value in every way, as it holds promise for the present life and also for the life to come" (I Tim. 4:8).

Fathers (6:4). Fathers have a moral obligation to their children which is also twofold. On the negative side they are told: "do not provoke your children to anger." It is very difficult for fathers to find the balance between softness and harshness in their correction of their children. In impatience and inexperience the best-intended firmness may give to the

---

[4] More details may be found in my forthcoming book, *The Hope of Glory*, ch. 2.

child the feeling that he has been crushed or that the father has been unfair. Such parental relations may lead to tragedy. A child does not become angry as long as he thinks his father is fair, but there is a point of provocation that does damage to the father-child relation. Here is indeed a place where parents and children alike need to hear the commandment of love which says: "Be angry but do not sin; do not let the sun go down on your anger" (Eph. 4:26).

On the positive side the fathers are instructed to "bring them [the children] up in the discipline and instruction of the Lord" (6:4). This statement may be given a negative interpretation also, for the words may have reference to corporal punishment and oral rebuke. In the LXX *paideia* (discipline) usually means "chastisement" (cf. Heb. 12:11), and the cognate verb *paideuō* is used by Paul to mean chastise (I Cor. 11:32; II Cor. 6:9). *Nouthesia* (instruction) would then mean rebuke, and the Christian view would be the same as the *patria potestas* of Roman law which gave the father absolute dominion over his child.

It seems, however, that the present passage has a more positive meaning. A few verses above (5:29) the verb *ektrephō* (bring up) was used in relation to *thalpō* (cherish) to describe how a husband should, in all tenderness, nourish and cherish his wife (*ektrephei kai thalpei*), and there is no good reason to adopt a different meaning here (*ektrephete*, bring them up). The father is to have the same tender care for his children as he would have when he loves his wife as himself.

If this be the correct interpretation of the verb, the two nouns take on a tender meaning. Werner Jaeger has written one of the classics of education under the title *Paideia: Ideals of Greek Culture*, for *paideia* had the meaning of general education for children in Greek society. It is possible that the word is used in much the same way here to give a beginning to Christian education.

The religious education of the child rapidly becomes one of the pressing problems of the Church, and these instructions on the Christian household furnish a good foundation for further study and application. How and what does the Church teach the child before and after adolescence begins? If a child can be "saved" only when he is "lost," then when is a child lost and when should the Church expect him to experience salvation and present himself for baptism? Should the Church baptize infants born into a Christian household and teach them the meaning of their baptism when they can learn, or should they first learn and then come for baptism? These were the questions raised by Tertullian (*De Baptismo, De Anima*) in the early Church and by Anabaptists and Baptists after the Reformation began, but only today have all Christians found it necessary to face them fully.

The place of the household in the education of the child was important in Israel (Deut. 6:7), and Christian faith has a heritage from the beginning that needs new emphasis. The first New Testament writing uses the father in relation to his children as an illustration. "For you know how, like a father with his children, we exhorted each one of you and encouraged you and charged you to lead a life worthy of God" (I Thess. 2:11f.). This is a picture of the *paideia* and *nouthesia* (instruction) of the Lord in both the negative and positive aspects.

SLAVES AND MASTERS
(6:5-9)

At first one is tempted to give little attention to a problem which belongs to a slave society, but at no place is the example of Christ more relevant to a social problem than here. An early hymn began: "Have this mind among yourselves, which you have in Christ Jesus, who, though he was in the form of God, did not count equality with God a things to be grasped, but emptied himself, taking the form of a servant" (Phil. 2:5-7). In a social system in which emancipation was impossible, what was a Christian slave to do in relation to his

master, and what was a Christian master to do in relation to
his slaves?

Slaves (6:5-8). The extensive instruction for Christian
slaves (cf. I Pet. 2:18-25; Col. 3:22-25) indicates the great
danger that could be created by the Christian cry for freedom. An untimely revolt could be disastrous for the tiny
cells of Christian life in the early Church as it was for the
Anabaptists at the time of the Reformation.[5] The boundary
between reformation and revolution is always dangerous and
difficult to determine.

The conduct of a Christian slave is to be guided by
the principle of reverence for Christ. Three times in the
sentence this is emphasized: *hōs tō Christō* (as to Christ),
hōs douloi tou Christou (as slaves of Christ), *hōs tō Kuriō*
(as to the Lord).

The first part instructs them to "be obedient to those who
are your earthly masters, with fear and trembling, in singleness of heart, as to Christ" (5:5). Earthly masters are only
masters "according to the flesh" (*kata sarka*), but the slaves
are to obey them out of reverence for Christ. Obedience to
earthly masters does not destroy the Christian life, for superior
social status does not determine spiritual advantage. The
obedience to the earthly masters is an obedience to Christ
whom the Christian slave serves "with fear and trembling,
in singleness of heart." With all moral seriousness and un-
divided loyalty he is to obey Christ by obedience to his
earthly master. The ethical principle of reverence for Christ
reaches that far.

The second part of the instruction says: "not in the way of
eyeservice, as menpleasers, but as servants of Christ" (6:6).
Eyeservice (*ophthalmodouleia*) is the type of service the
master gets only when he "keeps an eye on" his slaves. When
the eye turns away the service stops. Menpleasers (*anthrō-
pareskoi*) serve only the men who master their lives, not

---

[5] George William, *The Radical Reformation,* pp. 362-386.

God who is above both. As slaves of Christ service is rendered out of reverence for Christ, not out of fear of man.

This third part speaks of "doing the will of God from the heart, rendering service with a good will as to the Lord and not to men, knowing that whatever good any one does, he will receive the same again from the Lord, whether he is slave or free" (6:6d-8). The religious motive in service is emphasized by the phrases "the will of God from the heart" and "with a good will as to the Lord." Affection and good will go a long way in making service a joy and a service for Christ. The motive of reward is often discounted, but the New Testament has no such restraint. The life one lives now, however much it may be lived for its own sake, has eternal consequences, both in reward and retribution.

Masters (6:9). Christian masters also have a moral obligation to slaves. The letter of Paul to Philemon on behalf of the slave Onesimus is a reminder of how the institution of slavery is transformed by a mutual recognition of the Lord, and the parallel passage in Colossians 3:22-25 reveals the personal and social standards by which this new relation was formed. Ephesians 6:9 builds on this background.

The Christian master has a reciprocal relation to his slave. As in the golden rule (Mt. 7:12), the master is to "do the same" for the slave that he would have done for himself. His slave is no longer a thing (*res*), a chattel to be bought and sold, but a person to be respected "out of reverence for Christ." Personal relations rule out all impersonal considerations.

Christian restraint, in which the Christian master is to "forbear threatening," is a logical result of the reciprocal relation. One does not hold a threat (*apeilē*) over the head of a brother that is loved. Threats destroy personal relations and put people behind a mask of insecurity and fear. Love removes these barriers and creates brotherhood.

Christian responsibility grows out of the recognition "that he who is both their Master and yours is in heaven, and that there is no partiality with him" (6:9). He who is the earthly *kurios* (lord, master) is transformed in his attitude toward his slave by the recognition of a heavenly *kurios* to whom he must answer for his human relations.

Christian regard for a slave rules out partiality (*prosō-prolēpsia*), favoritism. Religious revolution began when Peter learned this in his relation to Gentiles (Acts 10:34), and this was the basis on which Paul wrote recommendations to Philemon. "Perhaps this is why he was parted from you for a while, that you may have him back forever, no longer as a slave but more than a slave, as a beloved brother, especially to me but how much more to you, both in the flesh and in the Lord. So if you consider me your partner, receive him as you would receive me" (Philemon 15-17). It is reverence for Christ in the person of a slave that has made this radical change in human relations, even in a society of human slavery.

Chapter Six:

THE CHRISTIAN CONFLICT
(6:10-20)

One of the earliest writers this side of the New Testament, applying the concepts of this conclusion in the book of Ephesians, depicted the Church as an army and baptism as the act by which believers in Christ were equipped for combat in spiritual warfare (Ignatius of Antioch, *Polyc.* 6:2). Tertullian's treatise on baptism, which indicates that baptism and the laying on of hands were two parts of the same service, used a military word to designate baptism. *Sacramentum,* the pledge of obedience made by a Roman soldier as he put his hands inside those of his general, is repeatedly used. Christians pledge obedience to Jesus Christ as they symbolically die with him and rise to live the life of faith.

As long as baptism as a sign of forgiveness and the laying on of hands as a sign of the reception of the Holy Spirit were two parts of the same service, the soldier symbolism was a unity. The growing practice of infant baptism with the laying on of hands years later gave rise to the idea that there were two different sacraments: baptism and confirmation. The decisive writing was by Faustus of Riez in the fifth century. Faustus taught that infants were enrolled in the army in baptism, but they were not equipped for combat until they were confirmed by the laying on of hands many years later! A direct line leads from this through Pseudo-Isidore, Gratian, and Peter the Lombard to the standard statement of Thomas

Aquinas which did so much to establish the doctrine (*Summa Theologica,* Part III, Question LXXII, Answer I). It is therefore of great importance in current discussions to return to the idea of Christian combat in the New Testament.

In the last exhortation in the Ephesian letter the conflict between the Church and cosmic powers into focus. A call goes forth for Christians to "be strong in the Lord and in the strength of his might" (6:10). The power of "that working of the strength of his might" (1:19), which works in the Church through prayer, is adequate for victory. In this Christian warfare the Holy Spirit working through the Church opposes and finally conquers the devil who works in the world. Three steps are necessary for victory: (1) identify the enemy (11-13), (2) put on equipment (14-17), and (3) endure to the end (18-20).

THE ENEMY
(6:11-13)

The enemy's method (6:11). The Church is told: "Put on the whole armor of God, that you may be able to stand against the wiles of the devil. Wiles (*methodeias*) are schemes laid for spiritual disaster, the "deceitful wiles" (*methodeian tēs planēs*) in 4:14. Only the army of *alētheia* (truth) will be able to stand against these deceitful schemes, for truth alone can expose deception and defeat the devil.

Language of this type may sound strange to modern ears that have never heard the anguished cry of persecuted people, but it had a ring of reality to those who witnessed the death of martyrs, who endured after the example of the Lord Jesus. "In like manner they that were condemned to the beasts underwent awful punishments, being stretched on sharp shells and punished with various other forms of torture, that, if it were possible, by means of protracted punishment the tyrant might induce them to denial. For the devil devised many wiles against them" (*The Martyrdom of Polycarp,* II, 4).

Augustine's false exegesis of Luke 14:23 ("compel them to

come in") prepared the way for the devil's wiles to work in the Church. By the eleventh century capital punishment was used to put down religious dissent, and Pope Gregory IV committed the leadership of the dreaded Inquisition to the Dominican order. Thomas Aquinas used Titus 3:10 to justify the execution of all who cause divisions, since execution is the best way to avoid schismatics!

Protestants are not free from guilt in making use of the devil's wiles. Luther's treatment of the peasants, Zwingli's heavy hand on the Anabaptists, and Calvin's part in the burning of Servetus were as diabolical as any of the deceptive wiles of the Inquisition. If one reads *The Radical Reformation* by George H. Williams he will not be left without understanding as to why the "free churches" fear ecclesiastical centralization under state domination. The worst fanaticism is not too high a price to pay for Christian freedom, and the wiles of the devil can never be used to prepare the way of the Lord.

The devil looks for every opportunity (4:27) to deceive and destroy those who would witness to the truth. *Diabolos*, from *diaballō*, to throw across, describes him and his work, for slander and false accusation are means employed by him to destroy reputation, influence, and life. He is deceptive indeed when Christians come to deny his existence while they are being used as the instruments of his deceptive wiles.

In the Old Testament Satan, the adversary, plays an important role in the post-exilic period. He appears in the Lord's court to accuse Joshua the high priest (Zech. 3:1), stands before God to accuse Job (1:6-12), and instigates evil in I Chronicles 21:1.

In the New Testament, where the Hebrew Satan is often the Greek devil (*diabolos*), this dark and deceptive power is the adversary of God and the tempter of men. As men fall under his power they become the devil's children (I John 3:8, 10; John 6:70; 8:44). Although he has the power of death (Heb. 2:14), he will ultimately be destroyed (Rev. 2:10; 12:9, 12; 20:2, 10).

It is difficult for modern men, even those who have reverence for the Scriptures and know its content, to think seriously of a Satan or devil with whom they have to do. Yet experience in one's self and in one's society leaves deeds that can be attributed neither to God nor to man. In temptation a power not ourselves that makes for destruction often operates and one is made to wonder why certain things happen. A God of love is not the source of such experience, and man's will does not seem adequate before it. It is easy to brush this aside by saying that man blames the devil for what he did himself, but many intelligent people have admitted that this explanation is inadequate in their own experience.

In society as well as self this diabolical dimension appears. The horrors of Dachau can hardly be harmonized with the character of honest and pious German people whom one comes to know and understand. Americans may dismiss this with the remark that "Germans are just mean" until they themselves get involved in a race riot among people who were once devout and decent. Even religious hysteria often leaves a helpless feeling as all reason and order are thrown to the wind. Do not forget that the devil is still looking for an apportunity (Eph. 4:27).

The enemy's place (6:12). It is astonishing to read *where* the powers of the enemy are located. "For we are not contending against flesh and blood, but against the powers, against the world rulers of darkness, against spiritual hosts of wickedness in the heavenly places." In 1:3 heaven was the place of spiritual blessing, in 1:20 the realm of Christ's exaltation, in 2:6 the place where Christians sit with Christ. Some suggestion that evil powers may also be in this spiritual realm is found in 3:10, for there the Church makes known the manifold wisdom of God "to the principalities and powers in the heavenly places," but here in 6:12 it is the arena in which the Church wrestles against cosmic powers. This spiritual realm needs to be explored.

Metaphors of wrestling (*palē*) and war are mixed to describe a conflict which is not "against flesh and blood"

(blood and flesh, *haima kai sarka,* in the Greek), a human contest, but against cosmic powers that have become demonic. Four times *pros* (against) is used to emphasize the nature of this struggle.

The Church wrestles against (a) principalities (*pros tas archas*). Demonic powers are pictured as a political organization, and the first in rank are the principalities. At the end Christ will destroy them (I Cor. 15:24), and even now they are unable to separate those in Christ from the love of God (Rom. 8:38). Originally these were powers created in Christ (Col. 1:16), and Christ is their head (2:10), having conquered them in their fallen state through his cross (2:15). His headship in his exaltation (Eph. 1:21) is God's plan by which his manifold wisdom is now "made known" to them (3:10). As part of God's dynamic creation, which coheres in Christ, these powers, in their fallen state, need to be subdued so that the lost harmony of God's good creation can be restored.

These (b) *exousiai* (powers, authorities) are supramundane rulers and functionaries of the spirit world, always mentioned in the New Testament after the principalities. The relationship between these powers and the state has become a lively debate since the rise of the totalitarian systems that often come into conflict with the Church. Oscar Cullmann revived the double interpretation that sees the *exousiai* as both supramundane and mundane authorities.[1] According to this view the state as the servant of God, as in Romans 13:1-7, may become a "fallen state," as in I Corinthians 2:8. That which was intended to be "God's servant for your good" (Rom. 13:4) may, as "the rulers of this age," crucify "the Lord of glory" I Cor. 2:8). In Ephesians 6:12 these cosmic powers, in their fallen state, are behind earthly politics, and against them the Church is called into combat.

Christians in Germany were caught in a great crisis because Luther and his followers saw only one side of "the

[1] *The State in the New Testament,* pp. 56ff., 95ff. Romans 13:1-7 is discussed in detail by Clinton D. Morrison, *The Powers That Be.*

powers that be," and this has been the weakness of all Erastianism. Thomas Erastus (1524-83) of Heidelberg, with his theory of state supremacy in all matters civil and ecclesiastical, has given his name to one of the most perilous teachings in Protestantism. After his work was translated into English as *The Nullity of Church Censures* (1659), the theory was adopted by Richard Hooker in his *Ecclesiastical Polity* (1594), and this stands as one of the handicaps to renewal in the Church of England. One hopes it will not take a British Hitler to make all see what Thomas Helwys saw in his famous *Declaration of the Mistery* [sic] *of Iniquity* (1611-12), which protested the authority of the king in religious matters.

Third, the Church is called (c) to stand "against the world rulers of this present darkness" (*pros tous kosmokratoras tou skotous toutou*). This strengthens the "demonic" interpretation of *exousiai* (authorities), for both savior-gods and earthly rulers were called *kosmokartoras* in antiquity. The gods Serapis, Isis, Mithras, Mercury, Zeus, etc. were indeed designated by this title, but so was the emperor Caracalla. Behind the throne of visible rulers were invisible cosmic powers, at times good and at other times evil.

The darkness over which these world rulers have dominion was apparently associated with the worship of the sun, and many common terra cotta lamps have representations of this idea. The importance of renouncing this darkness to become children of light has already been noted (5:3-14), and the later baptismal liturgies that required a renunciation of the *pompa*, the parade of people with their gods, are best understood against this background. One of the most impressive was called Tenebrae (darkness).

In the Johannine writings the battle between light and darkness is even more pronounced (Jno. 12:31; 14:30; 16:11), and the great crisis of history comes in the crucifixion of Christ, the Waterloo of the world, when "the ruler of this world" (1:5; 3:19; 8:12; 12:35, 46) is defeated.

The fourth and final power against which the church must stand is called (d) "the spiritual hosts of wickedness in the heavenly places" (*pros ta pneumatika tēs ponērias en tois epouraniois*). In the spiritual realm are "spiritual hosts of wickedness," the foe of the faithful, the forces of evil spirits. Both spiritual blessings (1:4) and "spiritual hosts of wickedness" (6:12) are encountered "in the heavenly places."

All this demonology may seem far removed from modern thought, but the more one ponders this picture in the light of the dynamic universe of modern physics the less strange the thought seems. Theology, to be sure, does not need to return to ancient astrology, no more than to ancient cosmography and chronology, but a philosophy of fate, such as grips many today, can be dispelled only by a theology of the Holy Spirit in the spiritual realm where there is faith and freedom.

The enemy's time (6:13). The time of the decisive conflict is "the evil day." In ancient astrology this term would mean the point at which man is under his "unlucky star," and he would have his "lucky star" to thank for a better day. In the Old Testament eschatology this would be the day of the Lord when it "is darkness, and not light" (Amos 5:18, 20), and that is the background of the statement here (cf. Mk. 13:24-26, 32; II Thess. 2:8-10; Rev. 16:12-16; 20:7f.). Only the panoply (the whole armor) of God can prepare one for this crucial time. "Therefore take the whole armor of God that you may be able to withstand in the evil day, and having done all to stand" (6:13).

THE EQUIPMENT
(6:14-17)

The putting on of the panoply of God is the second step in the Christian conflict. Polybius describes the equipment of the Roman spearman as follows:

> The Roman panoply consists first of the shield with a convex surface two and a half feet wide and four feet high; at the rim, its thickness is a palm's breadth. . . . Along with the shield there is the sword; this they carry on the right thigh,

and call it a Spanish sword. It permits a powerful thrust, and a mighty cut with either edge, for the blade is strong and firm. Besides these, they carry two javelins, a bronze helmet, and greaves. . . . Most of them wear also a bronze plate of a span's breadth each way, which they place over their breasts — they call it a heart protector; those who are worth over ten thousand drachmas wear instead of the heart protector a breastcoat of chain mail (History VI. 23).[2]

In describing God's panoply the javelin is omitted and the girdle and shoes added.

The girdle of truth (6:14). The girdle represents truth. The hope of Israel was focused on a Davidic king who would have "faithfulness as the girdle of his loins" (Isa. 11:5). Truth (*aletheia*) means the same as the Hebrew *emunah* (faithfulness), so the Church is called to put on the same equipment as the Christ, the fulfilment of the hope in the house of David. In Christ one may be equipped with the armor of Christ.

Christian truth is far more than an idea that corresponds to a fact. It is an act of disclosure, first in the person of Christ, then in the personal relations of Christians. Belief comes through hearing "the word of truth, the gospel of your salvation" (Eph. 1:13), and this "truth is in Jesus" (4:21). It should be spoken in love (4:15), for self-giving and self-disclosure belong together. Truth is the relation of love with one's neighbor (4:25), and the fruit of a life lived in light (5:9). In all of this it is that which is done (cf. Jno. 1:14, 17; 3:21, etc.).

The breastplate of righteousness (6:14). Righteousness also belongs to the Davidic king (Isa. 11:5), and the Lord puts "on righteousness as a breastplate" to bring victory (59:17). To withstand the cosmic powers the Church needs the very armor the Lord himself uses in the deliverance of his people from bondage.

The breastplate belongs to the day and may be called the righteousness of faith, and at one place it is so described.

[2] Quoted from the *Interpreter's Bible*, Vol. 10, p. 740.

"But, since we belong to the day, let us be sober, and put on the breastplate of faith and love, and for a helmet the hope of salvation" (I Thess. 5:8). Both passages build on Isaiah 59:17, and it matters little whether it is called "the breast-plate of faith and love" or "the breastplate of righteousness."

The shoes of peace (6:15). With the girdle of truth and the breastplate of righteousness are the shoes of peace. Isaiah 52:7 has the proclamation (cf. Rom. 10:15):

> How beautiful upon the mountains
> are the feet of him who brings good tidings,
> who publishes peace, who brings good tidings of good
> who publishes salvation
> who says to Zion, "Your God reigns."

A warrior wearing the shoes of the gospel of peace is an amazing contrast in the battle against the cosmic powers, but this is the way human hostility is conquered and the harmony of creation is restored.

The shield of faith (6:16). In I Thessalonians 5:8 faith was a breastplate, but the equipment has been extended from two pieces to six in Ephesians 6:14-17, so faith is now compared to a shield. This is the piece of equipment that protects the whole frame of man, as in the description of Polybius, and it is used to ward off "all the flaming darts of the evil one" (6:16, cf. I Pet. 5:9). Doubt is a flaming missile that will destroy the spiritual life if it is not quenched by a personal faith, a faith that is the commitment of the whole life.

Faith is a paradoxical shield, for it means dropping one's defences before God, open surrender of self to him who is the object of our trust. The shield of faith is the very opposite of the mask of pride, for it is victorious through capitulation.

The helmet of salvation (6:17). God wore this helmet when he went forth to deliver his people (Isa. 59:17). In I Thessalonians 5:8 it is "the hope of salvation," for Paul thought that the final victory was in the future (Rom. 13: 11-14). In Ephesians 2:8 salvation was described as a past event, and it is perhaps used that way in this figure of speech.

As has been previously pointed out, it is a process of salvation that is past, present, and future.

The sword of the Spirit (6:17). The Spirit is a soldier who takes the word of God in hand and fights against the fallen cosmic powers. The Davidic king was predicted as one who "shall smite the earth with the rod of his mouth, and with the breath of his lips he shall slay the wicked" (Isa. 11:4). Much of the same picture is here with the Spirit slaying the cosmic powers with his sword.

It is good to think of the Church as an army. In the early Church baptism was an enrollment in the army of Christ. As has been said, the very word *sacramentum* which Tertullian used so much in his *De Baptismo*, the first treatise on Christian baptism, was used in the Roman army to designate the oath of allegiance given by a soldier as he put his hands inside that of his general and swore to be obedient until death.

Already reference has been made to the *pompa* renounced by the candidates for baptism in the early Church.

> "In baptism the candidate drops out of this procession [*pompa*], he leaves the devil's camp, and enters into the camp of Christ's army."[3]

In the present state of the Church one is tempted to rewrite the great hymn, "Onward, Christian Soldiers." When the Church has been conscious of her great mission in the world her members have been able to sing with exaltation.

> *Like a mighty army*
> *Moves the Church of God;*
> *Brothers, we are treading*
> *Where the saints have trod;*
>
> *We are not divided;*
> *All one body we,*
> *One in hope and doctrine,*
> *One in charity.*

[3] Josef A. Jungmann, *The Early Liturgy*, p. 80. A splendid description of the pagan *pompa diaboli* in the widest sense is found in F. Van Der Meer, *Augustine the Bishop*, pp. 47-56.

Onward, Christian soldiers,
Marching as to war,
With the cross of Jesus
Going on before.

Today, if sung in truth, the words of William H. Hudnut would be more appropriate. We would chant:

Like a halting caravan
Crawls the church of Christ,
We are feebly faltering
Toward our sacred tryst.

We are all divided
Many bodies we,
Kept apart by doctrine
And lack of charity.

Careful, Christian pilgrim!
Walk in doubt and fear!
With the cross of Jesus
Bringing up the rear![4]

THE ENDURANCE
(6:18-20)

The third step in the Christian conflict is endurance to the end. Prayer for the Church and for Paul are requested, the first with the metaphor of an army on the alert (6:18) and the second with that of an ambassador active for his country (6:19f.).

The Church as an army on the alert continues to use the military language of a Roman spearman as four alerts for total spiritual mobilization are sounded. "Pray at *all* times in the Spirit, with *all* prayer and supplication. To that end keep alert with *all* perseverance, making supplication for *all* the saints" (6:18). These four factors are four of the fundamentals of prayer.

The first alert calls attention to the piety of prayer: "with

[4] Quoted from Chester Warren Quimby, *The Unity of Mankind*, p. 116.

all prayer and supplication," following the order in the Greek text. Jesus transformed three forms of Jewish piety (the giving of alms, prayer, and fasting) by turning attention from the outward performance to the inward motivation, but he did not preach that men should no longer give, pray, and fast.

It is clear that the Church continued to offer "supplications, prayers, intercessions, and thanksgiving" by "lifting holy hands," much as was done in the synagogues (I Tim. 2:1, 8), and indeed such piety pervades the New Testament. One does not discard the forms of piety in order to discover a new depth of meaning. "Religious people, students of religion, theologians of all creeds and tendencies, agree in thinking that prayer is the central phenomenon of religion, the very hearthstone of all piety."[5]

The second alert is the practice of prayer: "Pray at *all* times in the Spirit." Prayer as a form of piety often becomes dead by being too closely associated with certain "seasons of prayer" and forgetting the Spirit. Seasons of prayer were indeed practiced by the early Church (Acts 3:1; 10:9), as all spiritual life finds need, but prayer needs to be the permanent posture of the soul toward God.

The so-called desert fathers of Egypt attempted to deposit the prayer of the publican ("God, be merciful to me a sinner," Lk. 18:13) in the unconscious mind and to live constantly with this unconscious prayer. Benedict of Nursia (c. 480-550) later sought to sanctify all time by a schedule of eight periods of prayer each day, seven of them based on Psalm 119:164 and the eight, at midnight, on Psalm 119:62. One does not doubt the sincerity of these efforts, but the whole Church can never be composed of hermits and monks. It is necessary to maintain mental prayer in the details of daily life.[6]

It is certain that Paul had a very different thing in mind

---

[5] Friedrich Heiler, *Prayer*, p. 1. An excellent introduction to prayer in early Christianity may be found in E. G. Jay, *Origen's Treatise on Prayer*, pp. 3-75.

[6] The mental prayer of Russian piety is vividly portrayed in *The Way of a Pilgrim*, tr. R. M. French.

when he instructed his converts to "pray constantly" (I Thess. 5:17). In fact, he found it necessary to rebuke those who would not work (II Thess. 3:10). Prayer "at all times" is possible for all Christians as they do the daily tasks of life, but there is also need for withdrawal after the example of our Lord (Mk. 1:35; 6:31f., 46; 14:32, and parallel passages). Public worship and private prayer were normal in his life (Mk. 1:21; 6:6), and a departure from his pattern is a distortion. In prayer as in other practices there should be freedom (I Cor. 10:31; Rom. 14:5-9).

Prayer "in the Spirit" is parallel to "walk by the Spirit" (Gal. 5:16); both are possible in daily life. Seasons of prayer should never be allowed to quench the spontaneity of prayer, but desire for order may do this. The words of Paul are a permanent warning: "Do not quench the Spirit, do not despise prophesying" (I Thess. 5:17f.). His balance between Pentecostalism and prophetism has been sadly neglected in the history of spirituality, so that one finds it almost impossible to hold to both in modern Christianity. How inclusive he was when he refused to repudiate *glossalalia* (talking in tongues), even though the order of the Church required some regulation (I Cor. 12:2, 14-16). For the difference between spirituality and slavery was as different as the father-son relation is from the master-slave relation (Gal. 4:4-7), and prayer was the profoundest experience of the human soul (Rom. 8:26f.).

Prayer by means of the Holy Spirit is one of the four great truths conveyed by the phrase *en pneumati* (in or by the Spirit) in the Ephesian letter. God dwells in his holy temple, the Church, *en pneumati* (2:22); the mystery of Christ was made known to the holy apostles and prophets *en pneumati* (3:5); the church is not to get drunk on wine, but to be filled *en pneumati* (5:18); so prayer is supremely *en pneumati* (6:18).

On to the end of the New Testament this precious treasure in prayer is found. "But you, beloved, build yourselves up on your most holy faith; pray in the Holy Spirit; keep yourselves in the love of God; wait for the mercy of our Lord

Jesus Christ unto eternal life" (Jude 20). John was in "the Spirit on the Lord's day" when he received his "revelation of Jesus Christ" (Rev. 1:10, 11).

The third alert is a call to perseverance in prayer: "To that end keep alert with all perseverance." This is the type of alertness called for in the parable of the doorkeeper (Mk. 13:33, 35), and Jesus also applied it to prayer (Lk. 21:36). In Colossians 4:2, on which Ephesians 6:18 is based, the alertness applies to thanksgiving and the perseverance to prayer, but Ephesians 6:18 does not mention thanksgiving. This is of no great importance, but it does suggest that both prayer and thanksgiving are a persistent attitude of the heart, even though seasons of special prayer and thanksgiving in public worship greatly help in building this posture of the soul.

Perseverance (*proskarterēsis*) in prayer is abiding alertness, alertness that lasts to the end. The noun *proskarterēsis*, which is found only at this place in the New Testament, has nothing to do with "the gift of perseverance," mentioned often as "the perseverance of the saints," for this doctrine was first formulated by Augustine in his famous writing by that title in A.D. 429 or 430. Perseverance in prayer is a task, not a gift, laid upon all who would conquer the evil spirits of a fallen creation by the Holy Spirit of God.

The purpose of prayer is the building of the body of Christ: "making supplication for all the saints." Supplication (*deēsis*) defines more clearly the meaning of prayer (*proseuchē*). Prayer is man's approach to God, but supplication is to supply a great personal need, while intercession is for others and thanksgivings are for benefits already received (I Tim. 2:1). "Have no anxiety about anything, but in everything by prayer and supplication with thanksgivings let your requests be made known to God" (Phil. 4:6). In New Testament times an order of widows gave themselves to "supplication and prayers night and day" (I Tim. 5:6). Already this was a vocation for which they took a pledge (6:11).

In scope, this supplication includes all the saints. This is petition on behalf of all the members of the one body of Christ, the Church. It makes a difference in prayer and in the Church when prayer draws a circle so large that none who love the Lord Jesus in sincerity are excluded. This does not mean that one must "compromise cherished convictions," as is so often feared; it means that the whole family of God needs the prayers of all the saints.

It is unfortunate that "saint" brings to mind only those select souls who have left this life. Always in the New Testament it includes all members of the body of Christ, usually of those still living. The restricted meaning developed in Church history and the elaborate regulations of prayer offices have left so many sincere people thinking that prayer is only for people with Church vocations, so they go on through life asking professional prayers to "say a prayer" for them. This is not intended as a slur at the "professed" but as a lament at the little praying done by good and plain people. What a renewal of the Church will take place when all the saints "pray at *all* times in the Spirit, with *all* prayer and supplication . . . with *all* perseverance, making supplication for *all* the saints"!

As an ambassador ever active for his mission Paul requests prayer "also for me, that utterance may be given me in opening my mouth boldly to proclaim the mystery of the gospel, for which I am an ambassador in chains; that I may declare it boldly, as I ought to speak" (6:19f.). In Colossians 4:3f. prayer was requested for an open door, but here it is an open mouth.

The message of the ambassador is that of *logos* (utterance) and *musterion* (mystery). It is not enough to have an open door if there is no opening of the mouth to proclaim the word of God with openness and courage.

Among the later preachers to imitate the Apostle by the opening of the mouth to proclaim God's word was John Chrysostom ("golden-mouthed") of Antioch and Constantinople. He remains a model, for the word of God flowed from his mouth "like the cataract of the Nile."[7] It is no wonder that

7 Quoted by Chrysostomus Baur, *John Chrysostom and His Time*, Vol. I, p. 207.

more than three thousand persons, in a baptismal service that lasted all night, were immersed in the baptistry of the cathedral of Constantinople in A.D. 404.[8] Such is the work of God when the door is opened and men open their mouths to proclaim the word.

The *logos* (utterance) is not the empty words (*kenoi logoi*, 5:6) that gingerly avoid moral issues and sublime truth, but the majestic "mystery of the gospel." That which once was hidden in mystery goes forth as the good news (*euangelion*) of God to transform the present life and to kindle hope for the life to come. It is the proclamation of "the revelation of the mystery which was kept secret for long ages" (Rom. 16:25).

The mission of the ambassador (cf. II Cor. 5:20) was an extraordinary union of bondage and boldness. How strange the soldier must have felt about the unusual prisoner whose leg chain was bound to his body, for that is the meaning of *halysis* (chain). Purpose and providence transformed an imprisonment into a mission (cf. 3:1; 4:1). "For this reason therefore I have asked to see you and speak with you, since it is because of the hope of Israel that I am bound with this chain" (Acts 28:20).

A bishop of Antioch was later to follow Paul's example in another way. "From Syria to Rome, I am fighting with wild beasts, on land and sea, night and day, bound to ten leopards, that is, a squad of soldiers, who get worse the better they are treated" (Rom. 5:1, Goodspeed).

The boldness of his mission and the proclamation of the message are strongly emphasized by the noun *parrēsia* (boldness, freedom of speech) and the verb *parrēsiasōmai* ("I may declare it boldly").[9] Freedom of speech stands in strong contrast to bondage in chains, as an ambassador, inviolable to foreign law, is contrasted with a common prisoner. "I, Paul, an ambassador and now a prisoner for Christ Jesus" (Philemon

---

[8]*Ibid.*, p. 87.

[9] W. C. Van Unnik, The Christian's Freedom of Speech in the New *Testament*.

9). "And he lived there two whole years at his own expense, and welcomed all who came to him, preaching the kingdom of God and teaching about the Lord Jesus Christ quite openly (*meta pasēs parrēsias*) and unhindered" (Acts 28:30f.).

CONCLUSION
(6:21-24)

THE BEARER OF THE LETTER
(6:21-22)

Tychicus, a native of Asia, went with Paul in A.D. 57 to take the offering to the poor saints in Jerusalem (Acts 20:4). With Onesimus he was the bearer of the letter to Colossae (Col. 4:7-9) and is later mentioned as a messenger to both Ephesus (II Tim. 4:12) and Nicopolis (Tit. 3:12). As Paul's *agapētos adelphos* (beloved brother) he was both a *pistos diakonos* (faithful servant) and *syndoulos* (fellow slave) (Col. 4:7; Eph. 6:21).

The almost identical statements in Colossians 4:7f. and Ephesians 6:21f. prove little one way or the other as to the author. One commentary says: "It is hardly conceivable that Paul would find it necessary to repeat himself so meticulously, especially in a commendation of his messenger, where the form in which the words are cast is of no significance."[1] Another says: "The virtual identity of the two greetings is one of the weaker points in the case against Pauline authorship. Would not an innovator have varied it more drastically?"[2]

Paul's purpose in sending Tychicus was profoundly personal. "I have sent him to you for this very purpose, that you may know how we are, and that he may encourage your hearts" (6:22). Both are tasks of personal trust.

[1] Francis W. Beare, *The Interpreter's Bible*, Vol. 10, pp. 747f.
[2] Henry Chadwick, *Peake's Commentary on the Bible*, p. 984.

The Benediction

(6:23-24)

Peace and grace, the two keys of the benediction, combine the Hebrew and Christian blessings. Peace, the Hebrew *shalom,* has been a major theme in proclaiming God's purpose to unite all things in heaven and on earth by beginning with his people, both Jews and Gentiles, reconciled in the one body of Christ (2:14-18). "In Jesus Christ neither circumcision nor uncircumcision is of any avail, but faith working through love" (6:23; cf. 1:2f.; 2:18; 3:14; 4:6; 5:20). God as *Patēr Pantōn* (Father of all), Father of Christ by nature, of Christians by adoption, and of all things by creation, is indeed "the Father."

Grace, with which the letter begins and ends (1:2; 6:24), is the heart of all Christian blessing. "The grace of the Lord Jesus Christ and the love of God and the fellowship of the Holy Spirit be with you all" (II Cor. 13:14). It is pronounced upon those "who love our Lord Jesus Christ," but it is not clear what is meant by *en aphtharsia* (in incorruptibility). Incorruption is used as a synonym for immortality (I Cor. 15:42, 50, 53f.; Rom. 2:7; II Tim. 1:10), and immortal love has meaning. "So the epistle which opened with a bold glance into the eternal past closes with the outlook of an immortal hope."[3]

The question of the last phrase (*en aphtharsia*) is answered with the decision as to whether it modifies *charis* (grace) or *meta pantōn tōn agapōnton* (with all those loving). *The New English Bible* takes the first word and translates the passage:

God's grace be with all who love our Lord Jesus Christ,
grace and immortality.

This is possible, but the participle is nearer than the noun, and the RSV has followed the other rendering. With this the letter and this exposition may end:

Grace be with all who love our Lord Jesus Christ
with love undying.

[3] J. Armitage Robinson, *op. cit.,* p. 138.